JOHN
AND THE

IAN

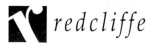

redcliffe

First published in Great Britain in 1996 by Redcliffe Press

British Library Cataloguing in Publication Data
A CIP Catalogue Record for this book is available from the British Library

ISBN 1 900178 20 6

REDCLIFFE PRESS
Halsgrove House
Lower Moor Way
Tiverton EX16 6SS
Tel: 01884 243242
Fax: 01884 243325

Printed and bound in Great Britain by Longdunn Press Ltd., Bristol.

JOHN CABOT: DISCOVERER OF THE AMERICAN MAINLAND

A FEW DAYS BEFORE the end of May 1497 the Italian merchant-cosmographer John Cabot and his crew of eighteen cast off from Bristol's harbourside. After letting the Avon river's strong tide take their little barque *The Matthew* gently downstream into the estuary of the mightier Severn, they put on full sail, and set course due westwards, past the last familiar landmark of Ireland's Dursey Head and out into the open, empty Atlantic ocean.

Some 35 days later they sighted land – land somewhere on the north-east coast of the continent of America. Although they could not know it at the time, the likelihood is that they had achieved what Christopher Columbus, for all his famous voyage of five years earlier, had not. Even following the two voyages Columbus had made to the New World as at May 1497, he had found only more and more West Indian islands. But Cabot and his men had reached what they would subsequently confidently describe as mainland. Mainland that we now know as North America.

On arriving, Cabot and his men did all the right things. Carefully choosing a suitable site for a landfall, they planted the Christian cross on the foreshore, accompanied by the flags of King Henry VII of England and Pope Alexander VI. Although they had no clear sighting of any inhabitants, several tell-tale signs, including the remains of a fire, left them in no doubt that there were living human beings very close by. Being few in number and therefore vulnerable to any surprise attack, they lingered only to collect fresh water before heading back to the safety of the ship. They then spent some thirty days exploring and charting the coastline, all this time staying on board *The Matthew* rather than risk another landfall.

On returning speedily to England and to the court of King Henry VII, Cabot argued confidently, with his Bristolian crew to back him up, that they had reached the Asian mainland – and with relative ease. All that was now needed was for a fully equipped expedition to make its way southwards from where they had been, and the spices and other prized products of the East could be obtained for a fraction of the cost of getting them via the traditional overland route. Indeed the necessary backing for such a mission was swiftly obtained, no fewer than five ships setting off from Bristol under Cabot in May 1498.

Had that mission returned successfully, even without having found 'the riches of Asia', there can be little doubt that the fame of John Cabot would today equal, if not exceed, that of Columbus. Biographies and travelogues would have been written, and dozens of statues and other monuments raised to Cabot's memory. In the event, almost nothing of John Cabot and of his expedition was heard of again, and in comparison to Columbus the name of John Cabot is little known.

So can the story of John Cabot and his *Matthew* even be written? Certainly after five hundred years it remains one of considerable mystery. But it is not a totally impenetrable mystery, as we are about to discover...

Detail from The Departure of John Cabot on his Voyage of 1497, *by Ernest Board, 1906. Some details of this reconstruction are historically unlikely. Cabot's doublet is too short, and his shoes too pointed for the fashion of the late fifteenth century. But his hair-style and clean-shaven appearance are correct.*

CABOT:
THE SURVIVING EVIDENCE

THUS IT CAME to pass that early in May 1497, a little vessel called *The Matthew*... sailed out of the port of Bristol and turned her prow towards the West... Never was a voyage of discovery, the consequences of which were so far-reaching, entered upon with less pomp and circumstance. Without flourish of trumpets or any outward demonstrations, Cabot and his English sailors sailed away into the unknown waste of waters. What dangers they encountered; through what storms they passed; what fears and alarms they conquered; what feelings gladdened their hearts at the close – of all these we know nothing.

Rev. M.Harvey

For the historian, one of the most serious difficulties presented by John Cabot is that, by comparison with Columbus, there survives so little documentary evidence for his life and for what exactly he achieved.

Admittedly, all is not clear cut even with regard to Columbus. Scholars still argue about his origins and about which West Indian island was the site of his first landfall. Nevertheless, there survive a detailed diary and letters by Columbus, together with several books he owned. His son Fernando wrote a full, supportive biography. Near-contemporary portraits provide a reasonable idea of his facial appearance. We know when he died, and where. Despite his Italian origin,

Spain adopted him as if her own, creating impressive monuments to his memory, as in Seville Cathedral.

Of Cabot, by contrast, there survives not the merest scrap of a diary, nor a single letter. There is no first-hand description by him of any voyage he made, existing even as a second or third-hand copy. No remotely near-contemporary portrait has come down to us. There is no certain knowledge of how, where or when he died. Of his three sons, Sebastian, the one known to have lived to old age and who followed his father's footsteps, seems to have been so keen to boost his own reputation that he played down anything his father might have done, and certainly did not bother to provide him with any biography. England, likewise, showed little inclination to provide him with any memorial, the few that now exist being mostly recent and of very indifferent quality. Even Bristol's hundred-year-old Cabot Tower has been more than a little neglected by comparison to its opposite number at St John's, Newfoundland.

Of the meagre contemporary documentary evidence for Cabot that has survived, none is in Bristol. The nearest, a rent book showing that Cabot and his family rented a house in Bristol's St Nicholas Street is kept 30 miles north of Bristol, in Gloucester's Record Office, and is not even on display. King Henry VII's impressive-looking licence authorising his voyage reposes rarely seen somewhere in the depths of London's Public

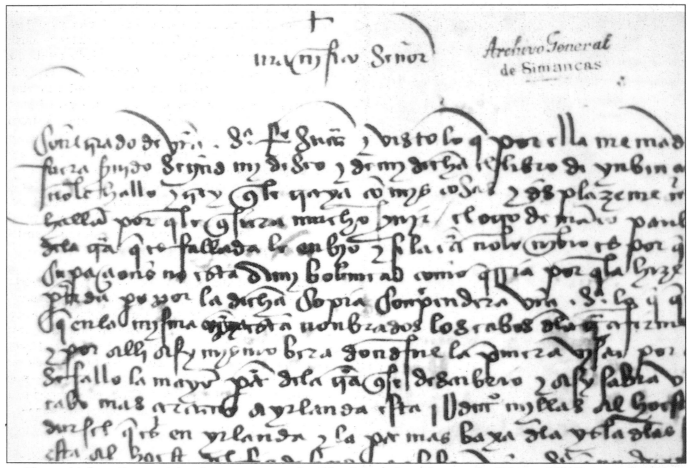

The most informative surviving document concerning John Cabot: a letter from an English spy, John Day, to a Spanish 'Grand Admiral' [thought to be Columbus] in the Spanish National Archives at Simancas.

Record Office. An accounts record of Henry VII's reward to Cabot is preserved in the Muniments of Westminster Abbey, but can be viewed only by special arrangement.

Further afield, Milan's civic archives preserve the report sent back by the Milanese ambassador in London who, while attending Henry VII's court, heard Cabot's description to the king of what he had found. Venice's Biblioteca Marciana holds a similar report despatched by Venetian merchant Lorenzo Pasqualigo.

But ironically it is Spain, the country with which Cabot was in most competition, which holds arguably the

Possibly Bristol's only physical relic of Cabot's one-time existence. This rib of a cow whale, preserved in St Mary Redcliffe Church, is said to have been brought back by Cabot from his voyage of 1497.

redevelopment. Some leading scholars are reasonably confident that this is the same John Cabot who then moved on to Bristol. As recently as 1955, in the Spanish National Archives at Simancas, near Valladolid, the American researcher Dr Louis André Vigneras came across what is arguably the most important surviving document concerning Cabot. This is a report by an English spy, John Day, informing an un-named Spanish 'Grand Admiral' – generally agreed to be Christopher Columbus – of every navigational detail that he had been able to glean from listening to Cabot describe his voyage of 1497 to the court in London. Although the report is undated, its content makes clear that it can only have been sent some weeks after Cabot arrived back from his 1497 voyage, and some months before his departure on that of 1498.

Additionally, Madrid's Naval Museum has a world map dated 1500, and signed by one of Columbus's senior crewmen, incorporating cartographical information that can only have come from an otherwise lost map made by Cabot during his coasting of the North American seaboard. Providing the map itself is genuine, and most scholars agree that it is, it seems conclusively to prove Cabot's priority as discoverer of the American mainland – and that Columbus was well aware of this priority.

It is to these materials that we will be repeatedly turning as the story of John Cabot, his famous voyage in *The Matthew*, and his mysterious disappearance, gradually unfolds. But first, why should John Cabot, by general agreement a man of Italian origin, have chosen to begin his venture from the English West Country port of Bristol?

most informative documentation. In the local archives for Valencia are records of a John Cabot Montecalunya working in the early 1490s on a proposal for a harbour

BRISTOL: THE PROSPEROUS MEDIEVAL SEAPORT

BRISTOL'S ORIGINS AS a seaport stretch back into the mists of the Dark Ages, but certainly even as early as the eleventh century it had achieved both importance and prosperity. William the Conqueror gave it its own mint and a castle on a par with the Tower of London. In the reign of King Stephen (1135-1154), it was described as

> nearly the richest of all cities of the country, receiving merchandise by sailing vessels from foreign countries; placed in the most fruitful part of England, and by the very situation of the place the best defended of all the cities of England.

In an age when cities needed fortifications for their own security, readily justifying Bristol's 'best defended' appelation was its location at the junction of the rivers Avon and Frome. In combination with William the Conqueror's carefully-sited castle, this provided a near-complete natural 'moat' to supplement the city's sturdy walls. Additionally Bristol was virtually impervious to sea attack because of the Avon river's unusually high rises and falls. Until the present 'Floating Harbour' was built in the early nineteenth century, any vessel visiting the city had to accept being completely marooned at each low tide – with all the vulnerability that this meant for any unwelcome intruder. As the satirist Alexander Pope (1688-1744) described it:

> ... in the middle of the street, as far as you can see, hundreds of ships, their masts as thick as they can stand by one another, which is the oddest and most surprising sight imaginable. This street is fuller of them than the Thames from London Bridge to Deptford, and at certain times only, the water rises to carry them out...

Adding to the difficulties for any would-be marauders were the Avon river's winding bends and strong currents, usually necessitating the help of the expert local pilots for safe passage to and from the Severn estuary and the sea.

All this made Bristol an exceedingly safe haven, and because it was also a natural regional centre, it attracted trade from both near and far. We are unusually well-informed about the city in the years immediately before Cabot's arrival thanks to a detailed Latin description drawn up around 1478 by Bristol-born antiquary William Worcestre, preserved at Corpus Christi College, Cambridge. From this we can readily identify many of the churches and other medieval landmarks that are still extant in Bristol, also a surprising number of the present-day street-names. We know that the best-heeled among the merchant community owned fine multi-storeyed houses on Redcliffe Street, overlooking the Avon river, that the docks boasted a crane, also that the mariners lived in an area of long-since drained marsh, marked by the still extant Marsh Street.

Also particularly evident is that there were some very good reasons for the phrase 'ship-shape and Bristol fashion' becoming part of the English language. Unlike many other European ports, in which those loading and

Simplified plan of central Bristol in Cabot's day.

unloading ships often had to wade through thick mud, Bristol's medieval forbears invested in properly paving their quay and building up the harboursides with free-stone to facilitate cargo handling. Rather than pay others to transport their goods for them, the more enterprising, such as William Canynges, developed their own ship-building industry. Vessels of up to 900 tuns – 'tunnage' denoted the number of 'tuns' or barrels of wine that a ship could safely carry – were constructed in the city's own ship-yards, the largest rivalling even the great carracks that plied the Mediterranean. Their hulls were made strong enough to stand cheek-by-jowl

Bristol merchants at the mayor-making ceremony of 1479. In the background can be seen King Henry VII's coat-of arms, as it would have appeared on the flag Cabot planted on his landfall in North America.

against each other on the Avon mud, and this also equipped them to withstand the rigours of anything from storms in the Bay of Biscay to icy seas in the North Atlantic.

From Cabot's point of view another of Bristol's natural advantages was that it faced west, particularly useful not only for the regular south-westerly voyages to Spain, Portugal and the Atlantic islands of the Canaries and Madeira; but also to Ireland and Iceland. And as we are about to see, Bristol's development of expertise in the latter voyages would have been of very particular interest for the intentions and ambitions of John Cabot.

HOW IT ALL BEGAN?

ALTHOUGH NO-ONE can be absolutely sure, there are some fragile but significant clues that Bristol ships may have reached what we now call Newfoundland several years before John Cabot had even thought of his transatlantic venture.

Quite definite is that from at least as early as 1436 Bristolian ships were regularly sailing the 1200 miles 'as the crow flies' distance to Iceland, voyages demanding far greater navigation and seamanship skills than anything normally needed by the Bristolians' maritime

Reconstructed Viking dwelling at L'Anse aux Meadows, Newfoundland. Excavations here in the 1960s revealed the remains of a Viking settlement abandoned within a couple of decades. The inhabitants had apparently been forced back to Greenland and Iceland by hostile natives.

counterparts, the Portuguese, the Genoese and the Venetians, all of whom preferred to hug coastlines wherever possible.

Navigating 'by needle and stone' the Bristolians transported to the Icelanders – descendants of Vikings who temporarily reached even as far as Newfoundland around 1000 AD – welcome supplies of good quality cloth, meal, beer, wine, longswords, silver buttons, knives, glasses, combs, etc. In return the Icelanders filled the Bristolians' holds with the one commodity that they could provide in plenty: dried cod.

For us today dried cod might scarcely seem the most exciting item of merchandise in which to deal. But before the age of the refrigerator and fast transport, there was a high demand for basic foodstuffs which could stand long storage. Properly 'cured' by the Icelanders' light salting and air-drying process, 'stockfish', as it was then called, could remain palatable for a year or more.

Additionally, because Europe was still predominantly Roman Catholic at the end of the fifteenth century, such 'longlife' fish was particularly useful for the Church's prescribed Friday fast days, for Lent, and for other days of abstinence. The great quantities of 'stockfish' which the Bristolians brought back with them even enabled them to onward-ship some as far as Portugal, where dried cod, suitably re-hydrated, remains a staple element in Portuguese cuisine even to this day

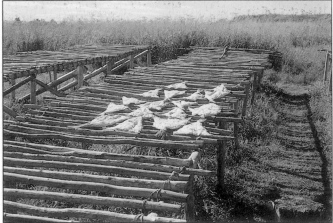

Cod being laid out to dry in Newfoundland, following the method of natural preservation the Bristolians learned from trading with Icelanders.

There therefore grew up a steady and amicable trade between the Bristolians and the Icelanders – only for this to be rudely checked in 1467. In that year the German-dominated Hanseatic League, who had acquired rights to Iceland as part of a European Union-type 'deal' with Norway, decided that they wanted to abolish the Bristolians' direct dealing with the Icelanders. This was in order to siphon off big profits for themselves as middle-men. Not unreasonably, the Bristolians objected, with the Icelanders backing them up. There then followed a classic international 'cod-war', with the Hanseatics driving the Bristolians away from Iceland with gunboats, the Icelanders being genuinely sorry to see the Bristolians kept at bay, and a pusillanimous English government in London getting nowhere via diplomacy.

Bristol's merchants were therefore left with two options. Either to abandon what had for them been a lucrative and much needed trade. Or to find a new source of cod, even if this meant learning the arts of salting and air-drying themselves.

One important indication that at least as early as 1480 they had begun looking for *something* far out in the westernmost Atlantic derives from one of the jottings of William Worcestre, the same individual who made the detailed survey of Bristol. This jotting notes that between July and September of that year an 80-tun Bristol ship part-owned by Worcestre's brother-in-law John Jay and captained by one 'Lloyd … the [most] competent seaman of the whole of England', had sailed far to the west on an ostensibly unsuccessful search for the 'Island of Brasil'. This semi-mythical Far Eastern island was the reputed source for the 'brasil wood' used for dyeing cloth a rich red.

The curiosity, however, is that only a year later two Bristol ships, *The Trinity* and *The George* came under suspicion from customs for carrying a large quantity of salt – apparently their sole outward cargo – on what their owners claimed to be another 'search' for this same island.

Now had any Bristol ship ploughed on past Iceland and found the rich cod-fishing grounds off the island that today we call Newfoundland, salt would have been the main commodity they needed to take with them. Furthermore, it is historically certain that the Bristolians *did* set up a flourishing cod fishing industry in Newfoundland, setting out with barrels of salt, and returning with Icelandic-style dried cod. But exactly how and when this began is completely undocumented. No-one can be sure, therefore, whether the Bristolians began this before or after Cabot's voyage of 1497.

Inevitably scholarly orthodoxy remains on the side of the latter, but one indication in favour of the former is that even as early as 1490, when as a result of a finally favourable English government 'deal' with the Hanseatics the Bristolians were invited to resume their trading with Iceland, they declined to do so, seemingly having already found an alternative source of supply. Another indication comes from the spy John Day's letter, which, in the course of imparting its 'secret' information on John Cabot's 1497 voyage, remarked in passing:

> It is considered certain that the cape of the said land [reached by Cabot in 1497] *was found and discovered in the past by the men from Bristol who found 'Brasil' as your Lordship well knows* [italics mine]. It was called the Island of Brasil, and it is assumed and believed to be the mainland that the men from Bristol found.

The riveting information here, from a very authoritative source, is that some significant time before 1497 – 'in otros tiempos', the Spanish words used by John Day, implies easily a decade or two – the Bristolians had already made a significant land discovery far to the west of Iceland, a discovery of which Columbus was already informed.

Although clearly we would like to know more of what lay behind John Day's statement, the implications for Columbus's own claimed priority as discoverer of the 'New World' are obvious. And such Bristolian success in westward voyaging would only add to the already substantial good reasons for John Cabot choosing Bristol as starting point for his voyage of discovery.

But who was John Cabot, that he should have even begun contemplating such a venture?

GENOA, VENICE OR GAETA?
THE MYSTERY OF JOHN CABOT'S ORIGINS

'JOHN CABOT'– for the normally accepted pronunciation, rhyme it with 'carrot' – is a mere anglicization of a name that originated as Giovanni Caboto. In Italian 'caboto' denotes a coasting seaman, from which it may reasonably be inferred that Cabot hailed from a well-established Italian seafaring family, though one in time-honoured Mediterranean fashion rather more accustomed to keeping in sight of land than venturing out into the open ocean.

Altogether more uncertain, however, is the city of the young Giovanni's birth and upbringing. According to

The city of Genoa in Italy, as shown in a contemporary woodcut. Some documents describe Cabot as Genoese 'like Columbus', but later he became a citizen of Venice.

the envoy Pedro de Ayala, writing to his masters King Ferdinand and Queen Isabella of Spain in 1498, Cabot was 'another Genoese like Columbus'. Genoa, on the north-western coast of Italy, would certainly be very logical for Cabot's origin, as it was a thriving seaport, just like its great rival Venice on Italy's Adriatic coast.

But there is also one document that suggests that the Cabot family came from Gaeta, near Naples. And one quite definite fact is that our John Cabot, while still 'Giovanni Caboto', was granted Venetian citizenship some time between 1471 and 1473. Since this was a privilege that could normally only be earned by having been based in Venice for fifteen years, the inferences are both that Cabot was *not* of Venetian birth, and that he must have had some strong connection with Venice since the late 1450s.

One quite definitely known connection is that his wife, whom we know to have been named Mattea, was a Venetian. Although there is no known record of her family name, or the year that she married John, this can hardly have been later than the early 1480s, since in a Venetian property document of December 1484 John is positively recorded as already a father of sons. Additionally, by 1496 John and Mattea certainly had three sons old enough to be accorded a mention in the licence that Henry VII granted Cabot for his voyage.

As a merchant interested in 'cosmography', Cabot undoubtedly shared with Columbus the belief that the riches of the East – so lauded by the Venetian traveller Marco Polo, and so difficult of access since the Moslem capture of Constantinople in 1453 – could be reached relatively quickly, and without the expense of umpteen middlemen, by sailing west. Indeed, far more than Columbus, Cabot seems to have had his own first-hand experience of the mysteries, and difficulties, of trading with the East by the eastern route.

According to a report by Milan's Ambassador to England, on more than one occasion Cabot had travelled to Alexandria in Egypt and even as far as Mecca in Arabia (to which he may well have gone in the guise of a Moslem pilgrim), in the hope of finding out where spices and other oriental commodities actually came from. In reality they came from the Moluccas, the Spice Islands of Indonesia, east of Borneo and south of the Philippines. But in answer to Cabot's questions, the travelling spice salesmen could tell him only that they did not know – that they obtained them from traders who had travelled from yet further eastwards than they themselves originated, and who in their turn did not necessarily know the original producers.

However, for Cabot, aware as he was that the world was round (despite popular supposition, this was accepted by most educated people of his time) this was all the encouragement he needed that the cleverest and cheapest way of getting to the Spice Islands and the other wonders of the Orient had to be by sailing westwards.

Even so, for Cabot the idea that he himself might try to make such a westward voyage might very well have remained just a pipe-dream – but for an unusual combination of circumstances ripe to inspire him to take it further...

COLUMBUS'S RETURN AND
HOW CABOT GOT HIS IDEA?

ALTHOUGH WE KNOW so little about Cabot, one city that we can be virtually certain that he stayed in a few years before coming to England was Valencia on the eastern coast of Spain.

According to Valencian local records, in 1492, the year that Columbus made his voyage to the West Indies, one John Cabot Montecalunya had been working on plans for an improved harbour. He is described as having 'designed and painted' these, and offered to supervise the constructional work involved. This John Cabot had had two interviews with the Spanish King Ferdinand, and at the end of February 1493 the king even sent his approval to Valencia's aldermen for the work to be carried out under Cabot's supervision. A month later, however, this decision was reversed when Valencia's local aldermen cancelled the project through lack of funds.

Now it was at about this very same time that Christopher Columbus, despite the loss of his flagship *Santa Maria*, had managed to return to southern Spain in the *Niña*, one of his two support ships. Swiftly journeying to Seville in anticipation of reporting to King Ferdinand and Queen Isabella there, he found that the monarchs had in fact made one of their occasional moves of the court to Barcelona. After all his sea travels this meant Columbus now had to journey some hundreds of miles overland to Barcelona, in the course of which one of the cities he had to pass through – with everywhere large crowds turning out to admire his captured 'Indians' and other 'trophies' of his venture – was Valencia. And it was just at this time that Cabot would have been still in Valencia nursing his wounds over the loss of the harbour works scheme, and wondering what on earth he could do next.

Now assuming that this John Cabot Montecalunya was one and the same as our John Cabot – and historians are in reasonable agreement that he was – he was possibly the one man in those Valencia crowds sufficiently well-travelled to know that wherever Columbus had reached in his voyage westward, the primitive 'Indians' and other 'Asian' trophies he was proudly parading were nothing like the true Indian caravaneers and other oriental merchants and merchandise that he had almost inevitably seen in Mecca.

Accordingly it may not be stretching history too much to suggest that Cabot, recognizing that Columbus simply could not have reached the true Asia of the Great Khan, perhaps conceived at this very moment the idea for his project to replace the harbour works scheme of which he had been so cruelly baulked.

This was to copy Columbus in seeking Asia westwards, but to do so by choosing a route along a latitude significantly more to the north, and thereby possibly succeeding where Columbus had so far failed. But first Cabot, like Columbus before him, needed both funding and some well-chosen royal backing.

CABOT AT THE COURT
OF KING HENRY VII

ACCORDING TO THE London-based Spanish envoy Pedro de Ayala, before venturing to England John Cabot had been 'in Seville and Lisbon seeking to obtain persons to aid him' in his venture. He was rejected by both, and although we are not told the exact reasons for this, they are not too difficult to guess. Spain's would have been because of the exclusivity of its contract with Columbus, from whom success was still expected, despite the setbacks he had encountered. Portugal's would have been because of the danger of breaching the Treaty of Tordesillas by which, under the auspices of Pope Alexander VI the undiscovered world had been divided between them and Spain.

So when Cabot eventually re-emerges in historical records we find him some time around the end of December 1495 or beginning of January 1496 at the court of England's King Henry VII in London. Here his presence was mentioned in correspondence between Ferdinand and Isabella and London's Spanish ambassador Gonzales de Puebla. This survives in the form of a letter of 28 March, 1496 in which Ferdinand and Isabella remarked in response to an earlier, lost letter sent by Puebla:

> In regard to what you say of the arrival there of one like Columbus [i.e. Cabot] for the purpose of inducing the King of England to enter upon another undertaking like that of the Indies, without prejudice to Spain or to Portugal, if he aids him as he has us, the Indies will be well rid

King Henry VII of England, c.1500.
[courtesy: National Portrait Gallery, London]

of the man … Take care that you prevent the King of England being deceived in this or in anything else of the kind…

In fact, despite Ferdinand and Isabella's warning, Henry VII had already come to a deal with Cabot, the terms of which had been drawn up in an official licence, signed by Henry on 5 March, 1496 and still preserved in the London Public Record Office. This grants

> To our well-beloved John Cabot, citizen of Venice, and to Lewis, Sebastian and Sancio, sons of the said John, and to the heirs and deputies of them … full and free authority … to sail to all parts, regions and coasts of the eastern, western and northern seas under our banners, flags and ensigns, with five ships or vessels of whatsoever burden and quality they may be … to find, discover and investigate whatsoever islands, countries, regions or provinces of heathens, in whatsoever part of the world placed, which before this time were unknown to all Christians.

Ponderous as the wording might sound, the careful stipulation that Cabot was entitled to sail the 'eastern, western and northern seas' in effect meant that the one route he was not authorised to take was a southern one. By this Henry VII, although not a signatory of the Treaty of Tordesillas, was clearly trying to avoid unnecessarily offending Spain and Portugal, Portugal already being a well-established trading partner, and the Spanish monarchs Ferdinand and Isabella being useful allies against the common enemy, France.

Even so, the licence entitled Cabot, on arriving at any new non-Christian land 'in whatsoever part of the world placed' to 'conquer, occupy and possess' all that he found. And for this reason alone Cabot's and Columbus's ventures would unavoidably find themselves in direct competition with each other.

Another difference, and one indicative of Henry VII's notorious thriftiness, was that the Cabot venture was to be 'at their own proper costs and charges', that is, at Cabot and his supporters' own expense. Also noteworthy was that Cabot was 'bounden and holden only to arrive' from 'our port of Bristol'. Probably this was exactly what Cabot, on casting in his lot with the English crown, would have wanted. But now the bond between Cabot and Bristol carried the force of law.

CABOT'S HOME IN BRISTOL

A S WE HAVE already seen, Bristol was the logical port for Cabot to choose as his base, both because it faced the direction that he wanted to go, and because its mariners had such well-recognised experience of navigating the open north Atlantic.

Although there is no direct evidence, most historians have not unreasonably assumed that Cabot must have set up base in Bristol some time before approaching Henry VII. This may have been so, but altogether more definite is the locality in which Cabot and his family lived for at least part of their time in Bristol. Preserved in the Gloucester Record Office is a rent book of the year 1498-9 in which among the rents paid to two Bristol property-owners, Philip Green (Bristol's sheriff in 1499-1500), and John Kemys, is listed 40 shillings (£2) from one 'John Cabotta' for a house in Bristol's St Nicholas Street.

From this we are able to pin-point in present-day Bristol the very street in which Cabot and his family lived. St Nicholas Street lies close to the River Avon at Bristol Bridge, though the old medieval stone bridge that Cabot would have known, and which was already 250 years old in his time, has long since been replaced. Indeed, because of redevelopment and the ravages of war, only parts of his parish church, St Nicholas's, are of medieval origin. And even this has been converted into a tourist information centre. Nevertheless, because of the parish system we can be virtually certain that St Nicholas's would have been the church which Cabot

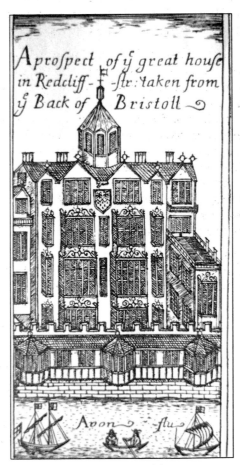

The sort of grand Bristol house a very wealthy ship owner might aspire to. Cabot's would have been much humbler.

St Nicholas Street, Bristol where John Cabot rented a house for his wife and family at the time of his voyages from Bristol. St Nicholas's Church is the only surviving building – and that only in parts – that Cabot would have known.

attended with his family. Adding to its appropriateness is that St Nicholas was the patron saint of mariners.

Also contributing at least a little to the information we have about Cabot is the Gloucester rent book's recording of the amount he paid his landlord. A rent of 40 shillings was significantly higher than that of most other tenants listed in the same rent book, though not as high as that of the Bristol merchant John Jay, who paid five pounds for a house in nearby Broad Street. Elsewhere Cabot was described as a 'poor man', a relative term, but certainly indicative that he was not conspicuous for his wealth.

It is far from certain that Cabot received generous or whole-hearted support from Bristol's close-knit coterie of merchants. Even today, Bristolians like to keep their city for themselves. And given the ambushing that one Bristol merchant, Robert Sturmy, had suffered a few years before at the hands of the Genoese, any Genoese arriving in Bristol would by no means necessarily have been welcomed with open arms.

As but one indication of this, it was common Bristolian practice for several merchants to band together for entrepreneurial ventures, thus sharing both the risks and the potential profits. But Henry VII's licence of 1496 notably lists not a single Bristol merchant, nor any named Bristolian, partnering Cabot in his bold venture. It may be that the documentation for this has been lost, or has yet to be brought to light. But it is also quite possible that Bristol's merchants, ever suspicious of 'foreigners', were concerned to keep secret for as long as possible their new source of supply of dried cod.

Accordingly, and while the scantiness of our documentation has to be stressed, the prevailing impression is that Cabot was essentially using the Bristolians' port, and was commissioning such of its men and resources as he could afford, for a venture that was largely if not entirely a London-sanctioned quest to reach the commercial heart of 'Asia', the real 'Great Khan's' Asia, before Columbus. It was a straight piece of rivalry to Columbus's, the one backed by the Spanish crown, the other at least sanctioned by the English crown, and both suffering from the same delusion as to Asia's nearness. But what sort of ship would the Bristolians, on the surety of King Henry VII's licence, provide for Cabot? Not least, would it be strong enough to cope with the rigours of a full Atlantic voyage?

PREPARING THE MATTHEW

Frustratingly, as with most of the ships in which Christopher Columbus sailed, all too little is known about the vessel in which John Cabot made his historic voyage.

We cannot even be sure that it was called *The Matthew*. The only known early document recording this name was the so-called Fust manuscript, a chronicle of Bristol from Roman times to 1565, the latter date being the year in which it was written or completed. Sadly this manuscript was destroyed in a bookshop fire in Bristol's Park Street in 1860, but thanks to the survival of a transcripted portion we know that it recorded that the Bristolians found America 'in a shippe ... called *The Matthew*'. According to one suggestion, by the erudite maritime historian Dr James Williamson, the true name may actually have been the *Mattea*, after Cabot's Venetian wife, anglicized by the Bristolians for whom there was no feminine form of the name.

If this is so, it would certainly be a pleasing mark of affection by Cabot towards his wife, perhaps highly necessary for having brought her such a long way from the warmth and splendours of her native Venice. It would also suggest that the vessel was either newly-built for Cabot, or specially adapted for his purposes, and then re-named, as had happened with Columbus's *Santa Maria*. In further support of one or other of the latter alternatives, no vessel named either *Matthew* or *Mattea* appears among the ships listed in the only Bristol customs record surviving from around the period of the Cabot voyage, that is, for the years 1492-3.

Of *The Matthew*'s size, all sources are in agreement that it was small. The Venetian merchant Lorenzo Pasqualigo called it 'a small ship', the Milanese ambassador Raimondo de Soncino 'a little ship, with eighteen persons'. John Day said it carried twenty. The Italian word used was 'navicula', usually translated into English as a barque, a common-enough cargo transporter during the Tudor period. John Day said the 'tunnage', i.e. the wine-carrying capacity, was fifty, making it about the same size as Columbus's *Niña*, which Columbus always insisted that he preferred to the larger, but more ponderous, *Santa Maria*.

The Matthew most likely had three masts. The mainmast would have carried the large, square mainsail that provided the main driving force for the ship when the wind was immediately behind, or just to the side. This also most likely had the crow's nest for the look-out. The rear mast would have carried the triangular-shaped 'lateen' sail useful for helping a ship sail into the wind. On the foremast there would have been another small sail for helping the vessel drive forward, and yet another on the bowsprit.

All the indications, therefore, are of a strong, fast, readily manoeuvrable vessel built in the best Bristol ship-building tradition. Even so, of exactly how, when and where *The Matthew* was built, whether specially for Cabot, or otherwise, we know all too little. Our only

The reconstruction of The Matthew *in progress, showing the ribs prior to being covered in planking.*

guide to her construction is what can be gleaned of standard fifteenth century practice from medieval paintings, engravings, old ship models, etc, and the occasional well-studied near-contemporary wreck such as Portsmouth's *Mary Rose*.

For instance, we can certainly be confident that almost everything would have been fashioned in wood, using tools that would not look out of place in a traditional carpenter's shop even today. When selecting the raw timber the shipwright would have been careful to pick

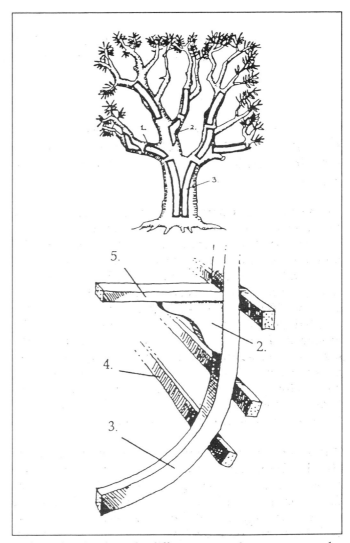

Plans showing how the different parts of a tree were used for different ship-building components, and how a medieval ship was constructed. The shipwright chose trees whose shape matched the requirements of the design. Key: 1 - floor timbers 2 - knees 3 - frame or ribs 4 - wales 5 - beam.

from seasoned and unseasoned wood as appropriate, and to choose those parts of a tree whose natural shape best suited his requirements.

For the keel, the very backbone of the ship, only the strongest and largest piece would do, usually taken from the main trunk of a mature oak. Laid on wooden blocks on the harbourside, to this would be attached the 'ribs', the uprights which give a ship its main frame. Selected from strong pieces of already naturally bent timber, each rib would be shaped, fixed in place with an inner keel or 'keelson', then further secured by cross-beams. These latter were in their turn fastened to the ribs by 'knees' – the ship-building equivalent of angle-irons – then strong timbers called 'wales' stretched around the ribs from stem to stern. Deck and side planking was then pegged into place using nails of wood, the gaps between the planks 'caulked' or filled with pitch-soaked hemp for maximum waterproofing, and the whole assemblage painted in bright colours, both for decoration and protection.

After the adding of masts, cordage, sails and general operational equipment, seaworthiness trials would then have been carried out, not least to determine the amount of ballast needed to give the vessel maximum stability. Many thousands of man-hours necessarily went into the making of even a small ship like *The Matthew*, but for the Middle Ages such cargo ships were of course the technological equivalents of juggernaut lorries and transport planes in our own time.

The Matthew *as she might have looked on the night before her departure in search of the New World in the summer of 1497. This imaginative painting by St Ives artist, Donald McCleod shows her moored below St Mary Redcliffe Church, minus the steeple which had fallen during a great storm some years before. The figures in the foreground are meant to represent John Cabot and son Sebastian.*

A FIRST ATTEMPT IN 1496?

Until Dr Vigneras's discovery of the John Day letter it had been assumed that the voyage of 1497 was Cabot's first attempt to cross the Atlantic. In fact it seems to have been his second. We also know that someone must have told Columbus about this first attempt, for according to Day:

> Since your lordship wants information relating to the first voyage [by Cabot], here is what happened: he went with one ship, his crew confused him, he was short of supplies and ran into bad weather, and he decided to turn back.

This can only have been a voyage made by Cabot in 1496, not long after Henry had granted the letters patent. We can have no certainty whether *The Matthew* was used on this occasion, or whether she had even yet been built. However an interesting indication by Day that there was by no means total accord between Cabot and his Bristolian crew is his information, which we will find repeated in another context, that 'his [Cabot's] crew confused him.'

Nevertheless John Cabot seems to have been nothing if not doggedly determined. If shortage of supplies was a problem on the first occasion, certainly, as events would prove, he would manage things better the next time. For as we can be quite confident from the historical record, by the May of 1497 he was ready to try again...

THE 1497 EXPEDITION'S DEPARTURE

No CONTEMPORARY WRITTEN or pictorial record survives of the Cabot expedition's departure.

For instance, we do not even know the exact date. According to the already mentioned Fust manuscript of 1565 *The Matthew* 'departed from the port of Bristowe [an old version of 'Bristol'] the second day of May' of our year 1497. But the spy John Day told Columbus that they left England 'towards the end of May'; also that they were 35 days at sea before their landfall which, according to the Fust manuscript, was on 24 June. If Day counted those 35 days from departing Ireland, this would have meant their leaving Ireland around 22 May, with their departure from Bristol (350 miles to the east), having possibly been on 20 May.

Similarly we cannot be sure even at which Bristol quay *Matthew* had been moored. It could have been St Nicholas's Back, now Welsh Back, hard by Bristol Bridge and close to where Cabot lived in St Nicholas's Street. It could have been just across the Avon river, from Redcliffe Back, overlooked by Bristol's richest merchants' houses in Redcliffe Street. It could also have been from Broad Quay on the River Frome, close to where today an uninspiring-looking plaque commemorates the event, and where the river has been covered over to allow an easier flow of road traffic around Bristol's 'Centre'.

Whatever, a fine oil painting created in 1906 by the artist Ernest Board (see cover and page 4) and now in Bristol's City Museum and Art Gallery conveys some-

thing of the last farewells, even if we have no idea whether Bristol's Mayor John Drewes and other civic and clerical dignitaries bothered to be present at all, let alone dressed themselves up in full finery for the occasion. Indeed the latter is most unlikely. All we can be sure of is that like any other vessel leaving Bristol *The Matthew* would have had to await a favourable tide to release it from the river mud and then transport it the six miles down-river to the Severn estuary and the sea.

In the course of that six miles it would have glided past the hillock now known as Brandon Hill, where stood a hermitage dedicated to the Irish explorer-monk St Brendan, now replaced by Bristol's memorial Tower to Cabot, completed in 1898. Past the hermitage *The Matthew* would have come to the imposing St Vincent's Rocks and Avon Gorge, at that time, of course, without its now famous Clifton suspension bridge. At the mouth of the Avon any guiding pilot would have been disembarked, and there would perhaps have been a final pause at King Road in the Severn estuary, a well-known safe anchorage for ships awaiting the right wind.

Then *The Matthew's* crew would have followed a familiar-enough course along the south Wales coast, across the Irish Sea, and skirting Ireland's southern coast. Finally, as the headland of Dursey Head, Ireland's 'Land's End', slipped below the horizon, the helmsman would have begun to follow the directions that only Cabot could give to sail due westwards, with the pole star on the right, out into the unknown…

No-one knows precisely what Cabot's ship looked like. Bill Bishop's painting of 1995 is based on a study of surviving information about other ships of the period – as is the actual **Matthew** *reconstruction by naval architect Colin Mudie. The original ship carried Cabot and eighteen crew across the Atlantic and back through storms and gales, and the hazard of icebergs.*

'35 DAYS BEFORE SIGHTING LAND'

THEY LEFT ENGLAND towards the end of May, and must have been on the way 35 days before sighting land; the wind was east northeast and the sea was calm going and coming back, except for one day when he ran into a storm two or three days before finding land; and going so far out his compass needle failed to point north and marked two rhumbs below.

John Day, writing to the Spanish Grand Admiral thought to have been Columbus.

According to the English spy John Day, John Cabot's outward voyage took him 35 days. As Cabot's crew would have anticipated, this part of the journey was bound to be the longer and the more difficult, because with the prevailing Atlantic winds blowing mostly against them, it would have been necessary repeatedly to tack to keep *The Matthew* on a westerly course.

Here is where the Bristolian crew's seamanship and navigation skills, and Cabot's own learning of the principles of navigation from his days in Venice, greatly needed to be honed into a good working partnership, one that all their lives depended on. As already quoted, Day specifically noted that *The Matthew* carried a compass, one which in conformity with the usual practice would most likely have been suspended on gimbals in a box in front of the helmsman.

Day also noted that in the course of the voyage *The Matthew's* compass exhibited a slight but significant

Ship's half-hour glass, as used to keep time on ocean-going vessels.

Astrolabe and compass.

deviation, a phenomenon that Columbus had similarly noticed back in 1492. This is a known anomaly prevalent at certain latitudes, and would have come to light because at regular intervals those in charge of navigating a ship checked their compass against the pole star, which in the late fifteenth century rotated around the true pole with a radius of a little over three degrees. By using instruments such as astrolabes and cross-staffs for measuring the angles between stars, together with nautical almanacs showing the stars' known positions for each night of the year, Cabot and whoever was the master mariner among his crew would have been able to calculate their position with quite reasonable accuracy. The main causes of difficulty were heavy seas, in which the astrolabe was impractical, and dense fog or cloud, in which the sun or stars could no longer be seen.

But because of the need to tack a sailing ship in unfavourable wind conditions, it was also of course necessary to make frequent adjustments to the course being steered by the rudder. To keep track of these adjustments a 'traverse board' was used, with eight holes bored along each point of the compass, each hole representing one half hour of a ship's 'watch', as measured by the half-hour glass carried by every ocean-going medieval ship. A separate line of pegs also recorded the estimated rate of progress. Although there was inevitably a certain amount of guess-work, the system was such that each four-hourly change of 'watch' could clearly see the progress made by its predecessor, and make any adjustments accordingly.

Sadly, whereas we know the names of more than 20 of the 90 who took part in Columbus's first voyage, the identities of those who accompanied Cabot have gone unrecorded. However, according to the Milanese ambassador Soncino, 'practically all [were] English and from Bristol', the exceptions, seemingly, having been an un-named Burgundian and a Genoese barber, this latter perhaps employed to keep everyone with the shaven chins that were the prevailing male fashion in the 1490s.

As already mentioned, Cabot's 1497 voyage, unlike its predecessor, would seem to have been reasonably well-provisioned, carrying according to John Day, 'food for seven or eight months'. As we will learn, only water was replenished throughout the whole outward and return voyages, and only with regard to the return journey was it remarked that supplies were running low. For food the staple fare would have been salted meat and salted fish (could this latter have included Newfoundland dried cod making its second transatlantic crossing?), together with biscuit-like hard bread and beer. To provide the occasional treat of fresh meat for Cabot and his senior officers live animals, such as chickens, may have been carried, though we are not informed of this. There may also have been a small barrel of wine.

With regard to sleeping arrangements, for ordinary seamen of Cabot's time and indeed for some centuries to come, there were no cabins as such. They would simply have had to make do as best they could with some chosen corner either below or on the single deck, depending on the weather. Of that weather, the spy John Day reported to Columbus that the sea remained calm throughout both the outward and return voyages, except for a single day's storm. In this they were clearly fortunate, and would thus have been in good shape when bird-life at last signalled that land was near, and a tree-clad coastline loomed on the horizon, just as John Cabot had said it would…

LANDFALL ON MAINLAND AMERICA

ACCORDING TO THE Fust manuscript, the Cabot expedition's landfall in America took place on 'St John the Baptist's Day', 24 June, 1497. This would have seemed particularly apposite for John Cabot, for whom St John the Baptist may well have been his name saint. The date itself may also be regarded as firm as anything we know about John Cabot.

Of Cabot and his party's impressions on their landing, all three of our main informants – the Venetian merchant Lorenzo Pasqualigo, the Milanese envoy Raimondo de Soncino, and the English spy John Day – provide vivid details. These they seem to have derived from listening to some form of lecture John Cabot gave to the English court on his return, also from directly interviewing Cabot. According to Pasqualigo, in a letter he wrote to his family 'back home' on 23 August, 1497:

> That Venetian of ours [Cabot, it is to be remembered, had acquired Venetian citizenship] who went with a small ship from Bristol to find new islands has come back and says he has discovered mainland 700 leagues away, which is the country of the Great Khan... [He] landed but did not see any person; but he has brought back here to the king certain snares which were spread to take game and a needle for making nets, and he found certain notched [or felled] trees, so that by this he judges that there are inhabitants.

The very same day that Pasqualigo sent his letter someone from the Milanese amabassador's office sent back to Milan a briefer note saying much the same, to be followed in the December by a much fuller account from ambassador Soncino himself, who had been away in the August. According to the main elements of this:

> He [John Cabot] started from Bristol... and having wandered for some time at length arrived at the mainland, where he hoisted the royal standard, and took possession for the king here [i.e.Henry VII]... This master John, as a foreigner and a poor man, would not have obtained credence, had it not been that his companions, who are practically all English and from Bristol, testified that he spoke the truth. They say that the land is excellent and temperate, and they believe that brazil-wood and silk are native there. They assert that the sea is swarming with fish, which can be taken not only with the net, but in baskets let down with a stone, so that it sinks in the water.

To this information the spy John Day added:

> He [Cabot] landed at only one spot of the mainland, near the place where land was first sighted, and they disembarked there with a crucifix and raised banners with the arms of the Holy Father [i.e. Pope Alexander VI] and those of the King of England, my master [i.e. Henry VII], and they found tall trees of the kind masts are made, and other smaller trees and the country is very rich in grass. In that particular spot, as I told your

Lordship, they found a trail that went inland, they saw a site where a fire had been made, they saw manure of animals which they thought to be farm animals, and they saw a stick half a yard long pierced at both ends, carved and painted with brazil, and by such signs they believe the land to be inhabited. Since he [Cabot] was with just a few people he did not dare advance inland beyond the shooting distance of a cross-bow, and after taking in fresh water he returned to his ship.

Despite the wealth of detail in all these three accounts, determining even within a few hundred miles exactly

Cape Bonavista, Newfoundland, thought by some to have been the landmark that was John Cabot's first sight of North America.

where Cabot may have first sighted land, and made his landfall, is by no means easy. On the present-day island of Newfoundland 'official' tradition has it that Cabot's first glimpse of the American continent was at Cape Bonavista, a very rugged and weather-beaten part of Newfoundland's north-eastern coast where, as this author can attest from direct experience, the rain can come down in torrents. According to the Newfoundland historian Judge D.W. Prowse, the very name Bonavista denotes its naming by Cabot:

> 'Bonavista! Oh good sight!' is the natural exclamation the old Italian [i.e.Cabot] might make as after his long voyage he first caught sight of land, bright and green with the springing grass of June. There is no other cape with the same name on the eastern shore of America.

Adding reinforcement to Judge Prowse's opinion there stands in Landfall Municipal Park at Cape Bonavista an imposing but lonely-looking Cabot statue erected in 1971 officially to mark it as the spot at which Cabot first set eyes on North America. Thirty-three miles to the south of Cape Bonavista lies Grate's Cove which one thinly-founded tradition claims as the site where Cabot landed and planted the flags. (Reputedly the cove's rocks even once bore an inscription carved by Cabot to commemorate the event, though few historians have been convinced by this). Further south still Cabot may have entered the superb natural harbour of St John's Bay, where Newfoundland's present-day capital, St John's, has a late-nineteenth century Cabot Tower twinned with that of Bristol, and (unlike Bristol's) complete with an excellent visitor centre.

But take the ferry over to Cape Breton Island, part of Nova Scotia on the American mainland and there you will be invited to drive on 'the Cabot Trail', billed as 'one of the most beautiful drives in North America ...

named after John Cabot, the great navigator and explorer who first sighted Cape Breton Island on June 23, 1497.'

Commemorative statue of John Cabot erected at Cape Bonavista.

Nor does the meagre information about the signs of human habitation where Cabot landed greatly help identify the location. John Day mentioned the landing party coming across a stick 'carved and painted with brazil', i.e. coloured red. But since many of north-eastern America's native tribes, including the Beothuks of Newfoundland, used red paint for ritual purposes (the very name 'Red Indians' derives from this practice) this fails to provide any real pointer.

Clearly, then, there is considerable confusion concerning where, even within a few hundred miles, Cabot might have made his historic arrival in America. So do our sources provide any further information that might shed light on the mystery?

The natural harbour at St John's, Newfoundland, into which The Matthew *may have sailed at the time of North America's discovery.*

'ABOUT ONE MONTH DISCOVERING THE COAST'

WE MIGHT KNOW so much more about where John Cabot first arrived in North America if only the Spanish archives at Simancas had kept the map that the English spy John Day provided for Columbus, along with his letter. According to Day, this map bore the names of 'the capes of the mainland and the islands', almost certainly as Cabot had himself charted them. Even so, Day helpfully told Columbus of what the map showed:

> ... you will see where land was first sighted, since most of the land was discovered after turning back. Thus your Lordship will know that the cape nearest to Ireland is 1800 miles west of Dursey Head which is in Ireland, and the southernmost part of the Island of Seven Cities is west of Bordeaux River.

Now this seems to be hard navigational information, and ought to be helpful. For instance, since Ireland's Dursey Head lies at latitude 51 34 N a straight line of latitude westwards of this leads roughly to Cape Bauld on the northernmost tip of Newfoundland, which ought thereby to be the 'cape nearest to Ireland' that Cabot referred to. This would mean that Cabot arrived only just a few miles from where the Norse, five hundred years before, had set up their short-lived settlement at what is now called L'Anse aux Meadows in northern Newfoundland.

Similarly the mouth of France's Gironde river, on which the French port of Bordeaux stands (thereby readily identifiable as Day's 'Bordeaux River'), lies at latitude 45 35 N. So if we again follow a line of latitude due westwards of this, the southernmost part of the so-called 'Island of Seven Cities' that Cabot claimed to have reached would be located roughly at Cape Canso on the eastern coast of Nova Scotia, only a few miles south of the southernmost part of Cape Breton Island.

Unfortunately, none too great a reliance can be placed on the accuracy of such stated calculations of latitude, whether deriving first-hand from Cabot or second-hand from Day. Late fifteenth century astrolabe and quadrant readings tended to be notoriously inaccurate, particularly when taken on the deck of a ship, as at least one of Cabot's must have been. Furthermore, Columbus for one was all too ready to lie about any such readings quite deliberately in order to mislead potential imitators and those spying for foreign governments. There is every reason to believe Cabot might have employed similar tactics.

It is also important to recognize that just because Cabot's discovery became widely described back in England as the 'new found land', this was by no means necessarily the large island of Newfoundland that we know today. Back in the sixteenth century the name Newfoundland was indiscriminately applied to the mainland as well. Furthermore nowhere do the Pasqualigo, Soncino and Day accounts mention the Cabot expedition encountering either fog or icebergs. Yet any vessel arriving at the island of Newfoundland around June would normally expect to find both.

Similarly, if Cabot had arrived at Cape Bauld and 'coasted' Newfoundland for the 300 leagues (approximately 900 miles) reported by Pasqualigo during the thirty days described by John Day, he could only have gone southwards. Alternatively, had he arrived at a southerly cape, he could only have coasted either south-westwards or north-westwards. Yet John Day said that Cabot's expedition made most of its discoveries 'after turning back' – i.e. seemingly heading back in an easterly direction, which would have taken them straight back across open sea to Ireland.

It is also important to bear in mind that Pasqualigo, Soncino and Day all insisted, undoubtedly reflecting only what they had been told, that Cabot had found 'mainland'. This is much more readily equatable with his expedition having moved gently eastwards from somewhere to the south, along the mainly regular

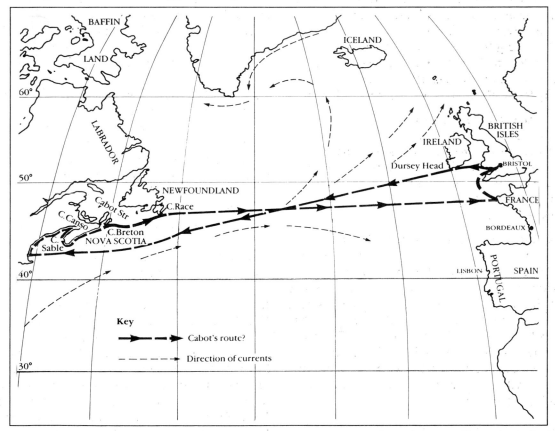

Cabot's most likely outward and return routes for the voyage of 1497, as reconstructed from information in the John Day letter.

The coastline of Cape Breton at Ingonish.

Given the stark alternatives of Cabot either having coasted eastern Nova Scotia or eastern Newfoundland, the discovery of the John Day letter has therefore had the effect of persuading many historians that Cabot may not have touched Newfoundland at all. It is possible that his first landfall was as far south as Maine, in which case Maine would have been his 'mainland', and Nova Scotia his Isle of the Seven Cities. But the more favoured view is that he arrived somewhere between Nova Scotia's Capes Sable (its most southerly point) and Canso, and then worked his way east north-eastwards along Nova Scotia. Here he would still have seen tall trees and cod a-plenty, and his departure point, Day's 'above-mentioned cape of the mainland which is nearest to Ireland', would then have been Cape Breton.

According to John Day, somewhere during their coasting those on watch on *The Matthew* saw two large, unwieldy creatures chasing each other. From the distance it was impossible to tell whether these were men or bears. Either way this adds little to the geographical uncertainties, but there is in fact one further clue that Cape Breton may have been Cabot's 'cape of the mainland... nearest to Ireland'. According to Pasqualigo's information:

> On the way back, he [Cabot] saw two islands, but was unwilling to land, in order not to lose time, as he was in want of provisions.

Had Cabot's cape of departure been Cape Breton, then the two main spurs of Newfoundland could well have been what he interpreted as two islands.

Whatever, the Cabot expedition's principal objective of finding what they could only assume to be the Asian mainland had been achieved almost with ease. Now they had only to get back safely to England to relate their news...

mainland American coastline. In this same context it is to be noted that John Day's words 'all along the coast', and 'following the shore' suggest a relatively continuous west-to-east type of coastline. This hardly fits the present-day island of Newfoundland, the whole coast of which comprises extremely jagged peninsulas.

IN HASTE BACK TO HENRY VII

ACCORDING TO JOHN DAY:

> From the above-mentioned cape of the mainland which is nearest to Ireland, they returned to Europe in fifteen days. They had the wind behind them, and he reached Brittany because the sailors confused him, saying that he was heading too far north. From there he came to Bristol, and he went to see the King to report [everything] to him.

For the return journey the Cabot expedition must certainly have 'had the wind behind them'. To have made the crossing in fifteen days was very fast on the part of *The Matthew*, even by the standards of the more advanced sailing ships that were used for the 'cod run' in the decades and centuries to follow. The information that Cabot's homeward course was too southerly, causing them to arrive off what would have been the island of Ushant off Brittany, is also interesting, arguably supporting the view that back across the Atlantic they had been perhaps rather more to the south either than they were prepared to admit, or they themselves supposed. Conceivably Cabot's crew's alleged 'confusing' him (for the second time, the first, we may remember, having been on the 1496 voyage), may have been quite deliberately to steer him away from their possibly already established fishing grounds in the present-day Newfoundland's myriads of bays.

Whatever, the island of Ushant off Brittany would have been already so well-known to the Bristolians as a navigational landmark that the mistake was quickly rectified, and their home port reached without further ado. According to the Fust manuscript the date of their home-coming was 6 August, which corresponds well with Day's information of a month's coasting, and a fifteen day transatlantic crossing following the original landfall on 24 June.

Cabot and his companions seem then to have lost very little time in Bristol enjoying their welcome-home before leaving hotfoot overland to impart their news to the royal court in London. Bristol lies 120 miles west of London, with 40 miles normally about the maximum distance that could be travelled in a day by horseback, given the rough roads. Yet by 10 August Cabot is recorded in King Henry VII's Household Books as gaining an audience with the King, and within as little as a fortnight the first reports by foreign courtiers were on their way back to overseas capitals. For the benefit of these foreign ambassadors Cabot may well have given some form of illustrated lecture, for ambassador Soncino reported:

> This master John has the description of the world in a map, and also in a solid sphere, which he has made, and shows where he has been... He tells all this in such a way, and makes everything so plain, that I also feel compelled to believe him.

But would others believe him? On the strength of his demonstrably successful exploratory voyage, would Cabot now get the backing for a fully equipped expedition with sufficient numbers and protection to be able to meet and parley with unknown 'Asians' without fear of murder or ambush?

A NEW, MUCH BIGGER
EXPEDITION PREPARES

ACCORDING TO THE spy John Day, reporting to Columbus:

> The King granted him [Cabot] an annual pension of twenty pounds sterling to sustain himself until the time comes when more will be known of this business, since with God's help it is hoped to push through plans for exploring the said land more thoroughly next year with ten or twelve vessels.

John Day's mention of the pension Henry VII granted to Cabot is an item for which we have proper, independent documentary corroboration. For in 1897, around the time that Bristol was celebrating the 400th anniversary of Cabot's voyage, a hitherto uncatalogued accounts roll of Bristol's customs for 1496-9 came to light in the muniments room at Westminster Abbey. This shows, among the outgoings paid out for the years 1498-9 by 'collectors of the king's customs' Arthur Kemys and Richard Ameryk a sum of £20 paid to 'John Caboot' or his estate.

We can also be confident that the ambitious plans for another expedition, as described by Day, were quickly implemented, albeit on a somewhat smaller scale than first envisaged. According to Spanish ambassador Pedro de Ayala, in a letter necessarily written in code to his royal masters Ferdinand and Isabella on 25 July 1498, a few weeks after the expedition had departed:

> The fleet he [Henry VII] prepared, which consisted of five vessels, was provisioned for a year.

London's *Great Chronicle* also helpfully recorded for the year September 1497 to September 1498:

> This year also the king by means of a Venetian which made himself very expert and cunning in knowledge of the circuit of the world and islands of the same, as by a chart and other demonstrations reasonable he showed, caused the king to man and victual a ship at Bristol to seek for an island which he said he knew well was rich and replenished with rich commodities. Which ship thus manned and victualled at the king's cost, divers merchants of London ventured in [her] small stocks, [there] being in her as chief patron the said Venetian. And in the company of the said ship sailed also out of Bristol three or four small ships stocked with small and large merchandise such as coarse cloth caps, laces, points, and other trifles. And so departed from Bristol in the beginning of May...

This *Chronicle* is our chief source for information on Cabot's 1498 expedition, and from it we know that the expedition sailed from Bristol very early in May 1498, and that for this Cabot was no longer on board *The Matthew*, which may well not have taken part. Instead Cabot was in overall command of a 'king's ship'. This was one apparently still hailing from Bristol, but in which the crew and provisions were all specially paid for by King Henry VII, who inevitably expected a suitable share of any proceeds. Of the other smaller vessels, it is generally assumed that some at least were Bristol-

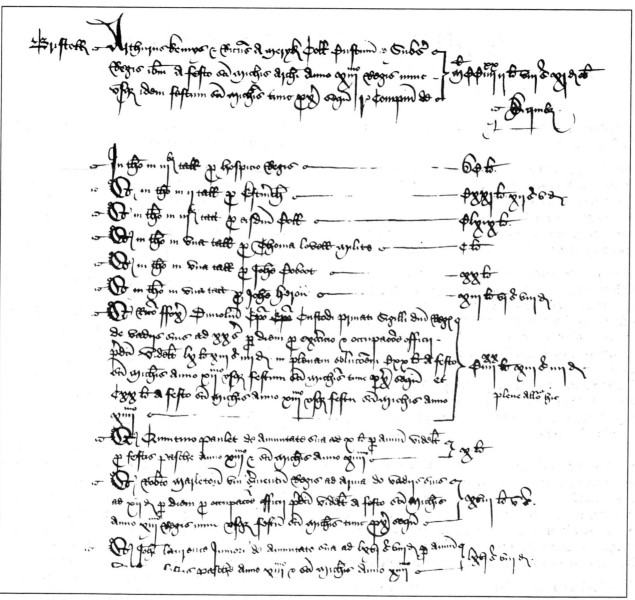

Henry VII's grant of a pension of £20 to John Cabot, to be paid from Bristol's customs receipts.

based and manned. But there is no certainty, the only definite information being that they sailed from Bristol and that at least a proportion of the merchandise with which they were freighted had been provided by London merchants.

The somewhat low-grade character of this merchandise indicates that, as in the case of Columbus, they were intending to dupe the 'Asians' with little better than baubles in exchange for the spices and other costly items with which they hoped to fill their holds for the return voyage. That spices were indeed their target merchandise, and that London was the city to which it was hoped to bring these, is evident from the earlier quoted letter of Soncino:

> By this means they hope to make London a more important mart for spices than Alexandria.

It is also noteworthy that Cabot's letters patent for this 1498 voyage, preserved in the London Public Record Office, no longer insisted on Bristol as the required port either of departure or return. Instead Cabot was now allowed to 'take at his pleasure six English ships in any port or ports or other place within this realm of England'. This suggests that this second expedition may have raised rather more enthusiasm in London than in Bristol, just as we suspected in the case of the first.

Unfortunately, as with the 1497 voyage, we know all too little about the people who sailed with Cabot on this expedition of 1498. Nonetheless a clue to just a few of these derives from entries in Henry VII's Household Books for Spring 1498, in which we find Henry bestowing some varying cash gifts on certain Londoners who are either taking part in, or sponsoring, the expedition. Thus for the period March 17-22 there occurs the entry:

'Item, to Lancelot Thirkill of London, upon a prest [advance payment] for his ship going towards the new Island £20'.

For March 25-31:
'Item delivered to Lancelot Thirkill going towards the new Isle in prest, £20'.

For April 1-3:
'Item, to Thomas Bradley and Lancelot Thirkill going to the new Isle, £30'.

For April 4-6:
'Item delivered to Thomas Bradley and Lance Thirkill in full payment of £108 8 shillings, £43.8 shillings'.

Then, for April 8-11:
'Item to John Cair going to the new Isle, in reward, 40 shillings'.

In fact, both Thirkill and Bradley are both found mentioned some years after the expedition as working for Henry VII, which may mean that either they chose not to sail on the voyage themselves, or that they were on the one ship which turned back.

Rather more ominously, among several indications to watchful Spanish envoy Pedro de Ayala that the 1498 expedition was a scant-disguised rival to Columbus's continuing efforts, was the undoubted fact that it included priests. Back in the previous December the Milanese ambassador Soncino had hinted at this with the heavily sarcastic remark 'I ... believe some poor Italian friars will go on this voyage, who have the promise of archbishoprics'.

That this intention had been actually implemented is quite evident from the fact that Ayala's information to Ferdinand and Isabella included that accompanying the Cabot venture was 'another Father Buil'. As Ferdinand and Isabella would have been well aware, Friar Buil was a Benedictine whom they had appointed to accompany Columbus's second voyage, with special responsibility for converting to Christianity all the inhabitants of newly discovered lands. It was he who at Epiphany 1494 celebrated on Hispaniola the first Catholic Mass known ever to have been held anywhere in the New World.

It is even possible with reasonable certainty to identify the particular 'another Friar Buil' who accompanied the Cabot 1498 expedition. On 30 June 1498 Agostino de Spinula, another of the Duke of Milan's eyes and ears at the London court, wrote to his master of

> ... three other [recently arrived] letters, one for Messer Piero Carmeliano, one for Messer Piero Penech, and one for Messer Giovanni Antonio de Carbonariis. I will keep the last until his return. He left recently with five ships, which his Majesty sent to discover new islands.

Not only was this Giovanni de Carbonariis one individual whom we can positively name as having accompanied Cabot on the 1498 expedition, he was undoubtedly a cleric of some importance. For instance, we know that nine years earlier he had been entrusted with conveying messages between Henry VII and the Duke of Milan. And in 1497 ambassador Soncino spoke of him as the 'reverend master' to whom he would look for advice on arriving in England. Only shortly prior to his departure on the Cabot expedition, the Duke of Milan had written him a personal letter, as a trusted confidant.

By any standards, therefore, when the royally sponsored fleet of five ships set out from Bristol at the beginning of May, it was in all senses 'ship-shape and Bristol fashion' for making contact with, and trading with, the fabled lands of the 'Great Khan', in a manner that had so far eluded the Spanish. We also know that the Spanish court was being kept keenly informed about this by its ever-vigilant eyes and ears in England. So how would they feel about this very real threat to their interests?

NEWS THAT THE SPANISH DID NOT WANT TO HEAR

GERMANE TO ALL this is the fact that as at the time of the Cabot expedition's departure in May 1498 Columbus had found only more and more useless islands inhabited by primitive, naked natives. This did not trouble him unduly because from his knowledge of Marco Polo's *Travels* he took them to be among the 7440 that Polo had described as lying just off the coast of the Asian mainland. But to his own and his Spanish backers' bafflement, he had found nothing of this mainland, or the rich realms of the Great Khan that Polo had so vividly extolled.

Just how sensitive Columbus was on this point may be gauged from the fact that during his Second Voyage, a voyage to which he had attracted many with the promise that he was leading them to mainland Asia, he resorted to one of his not untypical perversions of the truth. While on Cuba he had been told by the natives that it was an island, and in fact he circumnavigated it to within 50 miles of the point at which it should have been obvious to him and to every one of his crewmen that it was an island. Yet at this point, dogged by leaking ships and by low food supplies, and in a move that could only be interpreted as saving his face for his return to Spain, he despatched a notary to every one of his ships demanding that each and every officer and crew-member sign a sworn statement that Cuba was the Asian mainland. This forcefully advised:

> If they had any doubt or knowledge of it, then he besought them to declare it, in order that at once

he might remove the doubt and make them see that this is certainly mainland. And if any should contradict him at any time, there should be imposed upon him on behalf of the Admiral a fine of one thousand maravedis for each occasion, and that his tongue should be slit; and if he were the ship's boy or a person of such degree, he should be prepared for this penalty by receiving a hundred lashes.

In the event Columbus did not reach the true American mainland until his Third Voyage when he briefly touched the Paria peninsula of what is now Venezuela on 4 August, 1498, three months after Cabot's five ships had left Bristol. But ironically, Columbus happened to be so ill at the time that he did not recognise it as such. Nor did he go ashore to plant any flags, simply supposing it to be another island.

Now as we have already made clear, there can be no certainty that even Cabot had reached the true American mainland, although the evidence is increasingly in favour of this. In the case of Cabot, however, we can be reasonably sure that he genuinely believed that he had (even though, just like Columbus, he supposed it to be Asia). He had quite definitely also given others good grounds for believing the same. We know that this news reached Columbus, and in the circumstances it can hardly have been what he wanted to hear.

Accordingly what cannot be emphasised enough – confirmed as it is by the very real concern behind Ayala's ciphered letter of 25 July 1498 – is that as of that summer of 1498 Cabot and the English on the one hand, and Columbus and the Spanish on the other, both had their sights on exactly the same objectives. So far as both understood the world at that time, they both had the aim of achieving untold wealth for themselves, their sponsors and their royal masters by reaching Marco Polo's 'Cipango' (Japan) and wherever else that the world's spices came from, via what they believed to be a now proven westward route to Asia. The key indication comes in ambassador Soncino's previously mentioned report to Ludovico Sforza, Duke of Milan, as penned 18 December, 1497:

> … he [Cabot] proposes to keep along the coast from the place at which he touched, more and more towards the east, until he reaches an island which he calls Cipango, situated in the equinoctial region, where he believes that all the spices of the world have their origin, as well as the jewels.

Ambassador Soncino, it will be recalled, had directly listened to Cabot explaining his plans, and had studied the map and globe by which he demonstrated these. His information that Cipango was Cabot's aim is further supported by the previously quoted passage in *The Great Chronicle of London* describing the 1498 expedition's goal as 'to seek for an island which he [Cabot] said he knew well was rich and replenished with rich commodities.'

Also notable is Soncino's remarking, inevitably from what Cabot had told him, that Cipango was 'situated in the equinoctial region', i.e. within the tropics, exactly where Columbus, setting off from the latitude of the Canaries, had expected to find it during his First Voyage of 1492.

The Spanish sensitivity to the dangers, no less acute for the accompanying geographical ignorance, is quite evident from Pedro de Ayala's remark to Ferdinand and Isabella:

> Having seen the course they [Cabot's five ships] are steering and the length of the voyage, I find that what they have discovered or are in search of is possessed by Your Highnesses because it is at the cape which fell to your highnesses by the convention with Portugal.

Nor had Ayala shirked in his duty by not pointing out directly to Cabot the risks he was running:

> I told him that I believed the islands were those found by your Your Highnesses, and although I gave him the main reason, he would not have it.

All that Ayala did not point out to Cabot was just how closely he and his royal masters had been shadowing the Italian's every move, for in the very next sentence of his ciphered letter he makes clear his knowledge of the information and map supplied by John Day: 'I believe Your Highnesses will already have notice of all this, and also of the chart or *mappemonde* which this man has made'.

Ayala also ominously suggested what we have independently found reason to suspect, that in what Cabot publicly declared he had found, as in his public 'lecture' to the London court, he had deliberately falsified the latitudes of his discoveries '… to make believe that these are not part of the said islands ['found by Your Highnesses' – i.e. by Columbus]'.

The Spanish, then, had good reason to be alarmed by what they had learned of Cabot's intentions. But what were they actually going to *do* about it?

45

LOST AT SEA? OR DID CABOT REACH AMERICA A SECOND TIME?

AGAIN THE SPANISH are our chief source for the information that serious trouble befell Cabot's five-ship expedition. Reporting from London, envoy Pedro de Ayala told his royal masters in Spain:

> News has come in that one of these [Cabot's ships]... has made land in Ireland in a great storm, with the ship badly damaged. The Genoese [i.e.Cabot] kept on his way.

The fact that Cabot's £20 pension from Henry VII is recorded as being paid from Bristol customs receipts for the year 29 September, 1497 to 19 September, 1498, and again for the same period 1498-9, was once regarded as evidence that he did manage to return. Today, however, the prevailing historical opinion is against this. We know that the expedition had been provisioned with sufficient supplies to last them for at least a year from the time of their departure in May 1498. So it was clearly intended and expected that they would be away for a long time, inevitably, to gain the maximum benefit from the venture. Furthermore it would have been perfectly legitimate for Cabot's wife Mattea or another senior member of the family to claim the money on his behalf while they believed him still alive somewhere overseas.

What seems to indicate reasonably conclusively that Cabot never did return is a reference to him in a manuscript copy of the *Anglica Historia* written by the Italian chronicler Polydore Vergil in 1512-13. Although by this stage Vergil could not even remember Cabot's name, simply leaving a space for it to be filled in later, he remarked of what can only have been Cabot:

> ... he is believed to have found the new lands nowhere but on the very bottom of the ocean, to which he is thought to have descended together with his boat, the victim himself of that self-same ocean; since after that voyage he was never seen again anywhere.

Even so, could all four unaccounted-for vessels, and Cabot along with them, simply have sunk without trace somewhere in mid-ocean as a result of the 'great storm' described by Ayala? Although this was certainly the opinion of United States' Columbus expert the late Admiral Samuel Morison, British naval historian Dr James Williamson has disagreed:

> In the history of Atlantic exploration for the ensuing century, beginning with the Corte Reals of Portugal in 1500 and going forward to Gilbert and Frobisher and Davis and the Virginian pioneers of Raleigh's time, there is no instance of a multi-ship expedition having been entirely wiped out by an unknown disaster; and we are entitled to say that the odds were heavily against it in 1498.

But if this was the case, if one or more of the four vessels which pressed on across the Atlantic actually reached the other side, what *then* happened to them? Are there any clues that members of Cabot's 1498 expedition did arrive in America? And if so, why did they seemingly never manage to make the return journey?

CLUES TO AT LEAST TEMPORARY SURVIVAL?

BESIDES THE ALREADY-MENTIONED intensive Spanish shadowing of Cabot's activities, it is important to remember that there was another party inevitably keenly interested in any 'Asian' coup on Cabot's part: Portugal.

By the Treaty of Tordesillas Spain had been accorded all undiscovered land more than 960 nautical miles west of the Azores, with Portugal being allotted all undiscovered land east of this. Portugal had therefore mostly concentrated on working its way slowly southwards down the African coast and then rounding this to reach 'the Indies' eastwards across the Indian Ocean.

In fact, within weeks of Cabot setting out on his 1497 expedition the Portuguese explorer Vasco da Gama had left Lisbon with this very intention. Unknown to anyone in Europe he was actually succeeding at this time, returning to Lisbon on 9 September, 1499, having reached the true India.

But meanwhile Cabot's excited talk in 1497 that he had found 'mainland' relatively near across the Atlantic – as little as 400 leagues west of England according to both Soncino and Ayala, and therefore arguably less than 300 leagues west of the Cape Verde Islands – could only in Lisbon cause interested speculation that this was likely to be on their, i.e. the Portuguese, side of the papally endorsed dividing line between the two territories. While the friendship between England and Portugal was much more mature and long-standing than any-thing that England would ever enjoy with Spain, nonetheless Portugal's Dom Manuel, as a successor to the exploration enthusiast Henry the Navigator, felt no constraint in issuing licences for his people to venture in the same direction that Cabot had taken.

One of those to receive such a licence was a fifty-year-old *fidalgo*, or gentleman of the Portuguese court named Gaspar Corte Real. In the summer of 1500 Corte Real set out and reportedly 'discovered' at about latitude 50°N (the parallel of northern France) 'a land that was very cool and with big trees'. Like Cabot, Corte Real seems to have taken a first, quick look, then followed with a major, three-ship expedition the very next year, 1501. Of this expedition Pietro Pasqualigo, Venetian ambassador in Lisbon, and brother of the London-based Lorenzo Pasqualigo who reported on the 1497 Cabot voyage, sent home a particularly detailed despatch on 19 October, 1501:

> On the eighth of the present month arrived here one of the two caravels which this most august monarch sent out in the year past under Captain Gaspar Corterat [i.e. Corte Real] to discover land towards the north; and they report that they have found land two thousand miles from here, between the north and the west, which never before was known to anyone. They examined the coast of the same for perhaps six hundred or seven hundred miles and never found the end, which leads them to think it mainland... They

have brought back here seven natives, men and women and children... They resemble gypsies... [and] are clothed in the skins of various animals, but chiefly otters... In their land there is no iron, but they make knives out of stones and in like manner the points of their arrows. *And yet these men* [i.e. the Corte Real expedition] *have brought from there a piece of broken gilt sword, which certainly seems to have been made in Italy. One of the boys was wearing in his ears two silver rings which without doubt seem to have been made in Venice...*

From much of the incidental detail given by Pasqualigo, including reference to 'very large rivers (almost certainly the St Lawrence)', there can be little doubt that Corte Real's 'mainland' must have been that of North America in the environs of the provinces of Quebec and Nova Scotia.

But the quite riveting item of information is the mention of the piece of broken sword, seemingly either proferred by the natives, or picked up by the Portuguese from the shore; also the silver ear-rings recognised as Venetian. For these items can only have come from one of the earlier English expeditions that had sailed from Bristol.

Of these, the still hypothetical pre-1492 cod-fishing voyages are the least likely. If the pre-Cabot Bristolians reached anywhere, this would have been only the present day island of Newfoundland. And we would not expect Bristolians to be discarding items of Italian manufacture, even though the 'Venetian' rings may well have been the sort of bric-a-brac sold in any European port.

Cabot's 1497 expedition seems similarly unlikely. As may be recalled, this made just one single landfall for flag-planting and water-gathering, hardly the circumstances for anyone to have inadvertently dropped both a sword-hilt and two silver ear-rings. However, if it was the occasion, it would further corroborate that Cabot did indeed reach the American mainland during this particular voyage.

The only viable alternative is that the items came from Cabot's 1498 expedition – i.e. that one or more ships did survive the storm and reach the other side. Yet even this possibility raises more questions than it answers.

For instance, did the surviving ships land up on the shores of Nova Scotia, only for the crewmen then to be murdered by the natives, and their belongings plundered? Could the sword perhaps even have been Cabot's own, broken during a last desperate skirmish. But if so, why should the same natives have shown no similar hostility towards the Portuguese on their arrival?

Alternatively, might Cabot's expedition have arrived peacably and in good order, and simply used the sword hilt and rings – the very sort of 'trifles' with which the Londoners reportedly stocked Cabot's ships – to barter for food or furs before making their way further south? On its own, without any more evidence to back it up, this latter possibility might seem still very tenuous. But, as we are about to see there is fragile but nonetheless significant evidence, again from the still all-too-little plumbed Spanish archives, that at this very time a mysterious party of Englishmen did indeed move further south...

'CERTAIN ENGLISHMEN'
IN SOUTH AMERICA?

Not long after King Ferdinand and Queen Isabella of Spain received their envoy's coded warning concerning the rival intentions of Cabot's 1498 expedition, there also arrived by messenger boat from the West Indies some depressingly bad news from Columbus. Still on his third and least successful transatlantic voyage, he was becoming so bogged down by sickness and rebellion that he would eventually be stripped of his command and brought back to Spain in chains. If Cabot was to be checked in stealing a march on Spanish ambitions, it would have to be by someone other than Columbus.

Here the wily Spanish monarchs had a real 'wild card' in the person of a ruthless and buccaneering cut-throat

The Caribbean coast of South America, showing Coquibaçoa, and the route taken by the Hojeda/La Cosa/Vespucci voyage of 1499.

named Alonso de Hojeda. Illicitly supplied by someone in high authority with copies of Columbus's maps, in May 1499 Hojeda set off westwards with a fleet of three ships, accompanied by Florentine opportunist Amerigo Vespucci (then on his first venture across the Atlantic), and Columbus veteran Juan de la Cosa. Having behaved unspeakably even on stopping-over in the Canaries, Hojeda's expedition reached South America and worked its way steadily along the coast northwards, 'killing, robbing and fighting' peacable natives along the way. Only when they reached what is now eastern Colombia, by a gulf the local people called Coquibaçoa, did they cease their coastal marauding and sail northwards to the Spanish base on Hispaniola for badly needed supplies and repairs.

Now from what is known of the timing of Hojeda's expedition, he and his fellow-pirates can only have been at Coquibaçoa some time around the August of 1499, only a little over a year after the storm-damaged Cabot ship which turned back had its last sighting of its four companion vessels pressing on relentlessly westwards. In which regard, of no little fascination is an authoritative-seeming statement by the distinguished early-nineteenth century Spanish historian Martin Fernandez de Navarrete, writing in his definitive history of the Spanish voyages of discovery:

> It is certain that Hojeda in his first voyage [that of 1499] encountered *certain Englishmen* in the vicinity of Coquibaçoa.

This statement has to be one of the most tantalisingly enigmatic in the whole history of America's discovery, all the more so because of the insistent words 'it is certain', and because Navarrete, noted for his concern for factual accuracy, and for the most diligent researches among the vast Spanish archives, uncharacteristically omitted to quote his sources in this particular instance.

If the statement is indeed to be believed, and Navarrete had some source which has yet to come to light, the only available explanation is that some members of Cabot's 1498 expedition not only reached North America for the second time, but then continued making their way steadily southwards a very considerable way down the eastern American coastline, all the while diligently searching, like Columbus, for Marco Polo's 'Cipango … in the equinoctial region'.

Tantalisingly, had they indeed done so they would have been bound to have acquired a far more extensive understanding of America's geography than any other Europeans at this time. Their wanderings southwards could only have convinced them that this had to be a whole new continent, just as Hojeda's men coasting northwards, despite their marauding, had gained corresponding knowledge of America's equally impressive southern half.

But the all too chilling aspect is that on meeting Hojeda and his Spanish desperados, whatever luck any Cabot expedition survivors might previously have enjoyed would very quickly have run out. Hojeda's well-attested ruthlessness towards South American natives and even fellow-Spaniards is indication enough that he and his men would have had little compunction about murdering any stray group of Englishmen. Indeed, he could feel entitled to execute them with impunity, on the grounds that they were trespassing on territory already allotted to Spain.

While we have no way of being sure that such an encounter ever took place, if it did Cabot's men may well have been too weak to resist, enfeebled by the fevers and malaria endemic in this part of Colombia. Equally possibly they put up quite a fight, since it was immediately after their time in Coquibaçoa that Hojeda's ships needed substantial repairs.

Whatever, adding more than a little credence to Navarrete's information is the fact that when Hojeda returned to Spain about the summer of 1500, instead of being hung from the nearest yard-arm, as his many acts of piracy deserved, he was supplied with a fresh fleet, granted a licence to return to Coquibaçoa with the title of governor of the province, and instructed:

> go and follow that coast which you have discovered, which runs east and west, as it appears, *because it goes towards the region where it has been learned that the English were making discoveries*; and that you go setting up marks with the arms of their Majesties, or with other signs that may be known, such as shall seem good to you, in order that it be known that you have discovered that land, so *that you may stop the exploration of the English in that direction* [Italics mine].

Hard to avoid from this is the implication that the English had been 'making discoveries' westwards of this, that Hojeda had stopped them, and that he was now to follow this up by pushing further westwards in the region where the English had been, setting up the Spanish standard instead.

A further revelation from this same licence is that Hojeda had been able to show the Spanish sovereigns hard evidence of emeralds, pearls and gold that were to be found westwards of where he himself had explored, in which regard how had he found out about such riches? Could this have been forced out of the Cabot expedition survivors prior to killing them?

Intriguingly, on being presented with first specimens of the 'green stones' Hojeda's royal masters expressed their gratitude by awarding him a grant of land on Hispaniola worded as if for future services, when one suspects it was for ones already rendered:

> Their Majesties make you a gift in the island of Hispaniola of six leagues of land with its boundary, in the southern district which is called Maquana ... for what you *shall* discover on the coast of the mainland for the stopping of the English ...

Nor are Navarrete's cryptic reference and the specific mentions of the English in the Hojeda licence the only indications of some sort of encounter between the survivors of Cabot's expedition of 1498 and Hojeda's piratical expedition of 1499. Another is a tantalising map – again in Spanish possession – which seems to show that Cabot's charting of the North and Central American coastlines had been far more extensive than he could ever have managed during his 1497 expedition alone...

A MAP OF MYSTERY

SECRETED BEHIND THE scenes at Madrid's Naval Museum, its rightful place on public display taken by a poor quality, hand-made copy, reposes a three foot by six foot Spanish map of the world regarded by several distinguished scholars as the most important surviving evidence for John Cabot's discoveries.

The map turned up in 1832 in a Paris curio shop, and where it had been before then is not known. One important feature, however, is that it carries the signature of Juan de la Cosa, the Columbus voyage veteran and expert cartographer who accompanied Hojeda's voyage of 1499. Another feature is that it is dated 1500, and thereby incorporates information that La Cosa had learned only in the immediately preceding months, during his time with the Hojeda expedition. The third feature is that in the course of depicting the whole world as he had come to understand it as at the year 1500, La Cosa broke startling new ground. To the left of the map are the eastern coastlines of a great continent that can only be North and South America, its two halves correctly bisected by the Caribbean with its islands discovered by Columbus.

The La Cosa map is almost universally regarded as genuine, and as such is therefore absolutely priceless as the earliest known cartographical depiction of what we now know as the continent of America. As we might expect, the depiction is far from complete, due to the relatively limited exploration thus far. Even so the mystery it poses is how anyone – even someone of La Cosa's considerable travel experience – could by the year 1500 have acquired such extensive knowledge of the eastern side of both the north and the south American coastlines.

With regard to most of the South American (and West Indies) features the explanations are simple enough. The drawing of South America's coastline from Guyana to eastern Colombia is nothing more than we would expect from La Cosa having accompanied the Hojeda voyage of 1499. The accurate delineations of the West Indies are also explicable from La Cosa having sailed with Columbus on his second voyage; also from the fact that he would inevitably have seen the copies of Columbus's maps as supplied to Hojeda.

Of the West Indies, one as yet insufficiently explained feature is La Cosa's emphatic and accurate delineation of Cuba as an island. As we noted earlier, Columbus did not fully circumnavigate this on his second voyage, stopping just 50 miles short. Similarly, it may be recalled that all who took part in the second voyage, La Cosa included, had been obliged to sign a sworn affidavit that Cuba was part of the 'Asian' mainland. Since no one, on the Spanish side at least, was known to have visited Cuba since, La Cosa may have possibly simply guessed Cuba to be an island.

But a far greater mystery to the map (and one possibly carrying its own explanation of the Cuba delineation) is La Cosa's totally pioneering representation of the North

American mainland. Indisputably this shows discoveries that had been made by Cabot and his English companions. For instance, the sea off one area of the coast is specifically inscribed *'mar descubierto por inglese'* ('sea discovered by the English'). This same coastal stretch is also decorated with no fewer than five English flags. Historians mostly agree that La Cosa must somehow have received some surprisingly authoritative information of the discoveries made by Cabot, but the really thorny question is whether this derived merely from Cabot's voyage of 1497, or whether the map embodies unique data from Cabot's altogether more mysterious voyage of 1498.

Understandably, the safer money has been on the voyage of 1497. We noted earlier from the letters of the spy John Day and from Spanish envoy Ayala that the Spanish were quite definitely supplied with a secret map of Cabot's discoveries on this voyage. Intriguingly, Juan de la Cosa's inscription on the Naval Museum map showed he made this in Puerto de Santa Maria, the very same port as that from which John Day wrote his spy letter to Columbus.

Furthermore, the flagged area of English coastline as marked on the map can be seen to be between the latitudes west of Ireland, to the west of Bordeaux's river, precisely in accord with the description in John Day's letter. Again in accord with Day's letter, the named cape that lies furthest west seems to be called 'Cavo Descubierto', or 'Cape Discovery', readily corresponding to John Day's remark to Columbus 'you will see [on the 'copy of the land'] where land was first sighted, since most of the land was discovered after turning back'.

Now if the flagged area on La Cosa's map does indeed represent Cabot's charting during his 1497 voyage, then this incidentally provides the strongest possible evidence that Cabot's landfall was not on the present-day island of Newfoundland, but further to the south along the eastern American seaboard. For although La Cosa's coastline cannot be identified with any exactness, it is most certainly not that of a heavily indented island such as Newfoundland.

But the really curious feature of the La Cosa map, and one in which it is strangely both on its own and ahead of all other similar maps for some thirty years into the future, is its depiction of a continuous coastline extending southwards from the flagged territory accredited to the English, then correctly encircling the islands of the West Indies that Columbus had discovered, an encirclement broken only by a vignette representing St Christopher.

For it cannot be emphasised enough that no European is known to have touched the American coastline anywhere along the north of the Gulf of Mexico, until the Spaniard Ponce de Leon reached and explored some parts of Florida in 1513. Yet La Cosa, albeit without showing place-names, confidently delineated a continuous mainland north of the Caribbean islands and at approximately the correct distance from these. He equally confidently showed the South American coastline stretching considerably further westwards than the Coquibaçoa region which was the furthest that he and Hojeda had reached in 1499.

As particularly noted by the historian James A. Williamson, this section of the coastline also happens to be one of the most uncannily accurate of the whole map, even though La Cosa makes quite clear that his expedition did not explore this section of coast. Thus although he shows a long line of new place-names stretching all the way from Guyana, following the route

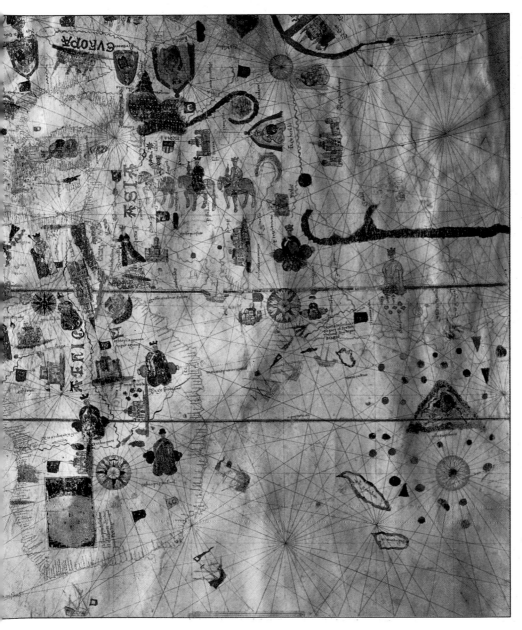

World map by Juan de la Cosa, dated 1500, showing North and South America, with the islands of the West Indies. Its particularly curious features are the five English flags shown along the coast of North America, and its near-complete Caribbean coastline, when most of this had supposedly not yet been reached by any European.

he travelled with Hojeda, this line abruptly stops at Coquibaçoa, terminated by an emphatic Spanish flag. Totally unexplained, therefore, is how La Cosa obtained information about the coast westward from this, a mystery arguably not un-related to how Hojeda obtained his information about this same region's gold, emeralds and pearls.

The key question is whether such features as marked on La Cosa's map could have derived from discoveries made by John Cabot and/or the survivors of his 1498 expedition.   Could these survivors have carefully charted everything they found on working their way south (inevitably planning to bring news of it all back to England), only for it all to fall into La Cosa's hands as a result of their fatal encounter at Coquibaçoa?

Strikingly in favour of the map indeed deriving from Cabot's 1498 voyage is the already noted fact that no fewer than five English flags are shown along the 'English' coast. Although five such flags should not necessarily be taken to mean five actual flag-planting landings, nonetheless they strongly suggest a much more significant and thorough English exploration of the coast than could be expected of the timid and perfunctory single landfall made by the Cabot expedition of 1497.

Similarly, while some of the place-names marked along the English coastline are difficult to read, none of them seems to bear any relation to those on Newfoundland, such as 'Cape Bonavista', that have been attributed to Cabot's 1497 voyage. This suggests that they were

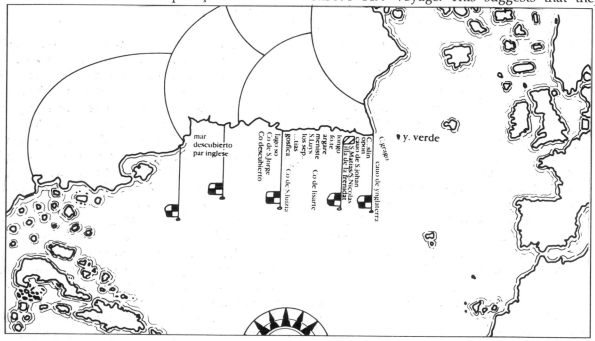

Section of North American coastline dotted with English flags — detail from Juan de la Cosa's map.

coined by someone who never survived to lodge them in the record books back home, precisely as happened to John Cabot and those who accompanied him on his 1498 expedtion.

But if Hojeda and his men did succeed in eliminating the men of Cabot's 1498 voyage, and taking over their charts, surely this would have become part of the public record in Spain? After all, the Englishmen had been trespassing into terrritories legally allotted to Spain, and thereby would have brought their fate upon themselves.

In fact, while privately Ferdinand and Isabella would certainly have approved any such 'stopping' of the English, as clearly indicated by the arguably retrospective licence that they granted Hojeda in June, 1501, undoubtedly they would also have been most anxious, particularly around the year 1500, that absolutely nothing of the story should ever be learned in England.

This was because of the very delicate and protracted negotiations, being finalised at this very time, whereby Ferdinand and Isabella's daughter Catalina (the future 'Catherine of Aragon') was to marry King Henry VII's eldest son and heir, the Prince Arthur. This marriage was to cement an alliance between England and Spain against their common enemy France. The months of 1500-1 were of the final intense diplomatic activity preceding Catherine's actual sailing to England in the August of 1501, and it would have been absolutely imperative that news of any murder of Englishmen by Spaniards, however well-justified, should not be allowed to leak to the outside world.

There is even some reason for believing that La Cosa's map may well have been prepared to justify the Spanish action specifically in the event of such a leak. As noticed by the historian Dr James Williamson, the map displays some curious falsifications of latitude, most particularly relating to the Spanish and English areas of discovery. Thus the coast shown as discovered by the English appears at a latitude only a little south of southern England. Then immediately to the south of this are shown all the Spanish-discovered islands of the West Indies. But instead of these latter being drawn at anything like their true latitude, they are shown as too far north by some twelve degrees, thus making any English wandering southward appear that much more of a flagrant trespass upon Spanish territory. In Williamson's words:

> La Cosa was a pilot of repute who had been three times to the West Indies, including twice with Columbus. He could not have made such an error in good faith.

Arguably, therefore, La Cosa's map was a deliberate 'cooking of the latitudes' to persuade somebody that any English movement southwards was seriously out of order. In which regard the date and location of its discovery in Paris in 1832 may have some significance, for less than a generation earlier the Emperor Napoleon, at the height of his power, had had the Vatican's 'secret archives' seized from Rome and taken to Paris. On his defeat some of this material was eventually returned, anything judged unimportant left behind to be sold by weight for wrapping paper and the making of cardboard. Could the La Cosa map have been specially drawn for the Pope, to persuade him that the Spanish would have been totally within their rights in the event of any blood shed in the protection of their interests? By Napoleon's time the map would of course have seemed long out of date and worthless. Was it therefore among the material discarded from the archives, then saved by some unknown Parisian because of its curiosity value?

In fact, even the La Cosa map does not provide the last word on the fate of John Cabot's 1498 expedition. For it may be remembered that besides Juan de la Cosa, the piratical Hojeda had a third companion on his voyage of 1499-1500, a companion whose very name raises questions about his rôle in the story of America's discovery. That name: Amerigo Vespucci.

HOW AMERICA GOT ITS NAME?

HISTORY IS FULL of accidents, and not least of these is that the continent of America should be so-called, instead of either 'Columbia' or 'Cabotia'.

Whatever our opinion of the two latter names, exactly how America became *seemingly* named after the altogether less worthy Florentine opportunist Amerigo Vespucci is not without its own relevance to the John Cabot story. As may be recalled, Amerigo Vespucci, whose background had been in banking and commerce, took part in Hojeda's 'stop the English' expedition of 1499 in a rôle that was little more than gentleman companion. To his credit, he does not seem to have totally approved of those among whom he found himself, for he left the expedition shortly after its adventures at Coquibaçoa, taking advantage of a ship that happened to be leaving Hispaniola for Spain.

He does, however, appear to have had his appetite whetted for transatlantic adventure, for in 1501 he joined a Portuguese three-ship expedition to Brazil, led by the nobleman Gonçalo Coelho, the chief achievement of which seems to have been the discovery of what is now Rio de Janeiro. Unfortunately what makes difficult any discussion of his genuine achievements is that on his return he proceeded to tell so many tall stories about his adventures that sifting the true facts among these is almost impossible.

For instance, in two letters to the head of the Florentine republic, given wide publication from 1504, he claimed

to have been on no less than four voyages. The first of these, under the Spanish flag, purportedly set out westwards from Cadiz in May 1497, 'reaching a land which we judged to be continental... distant westward from the Canary Islands about one thousand leagues'. The second one, also under the Spanish flag and which he described as setting out in 1499, seems to have been the genuine expedition led by Hojeda, except that Hojeda went unmentioned. The third voyage, which Vespucci dated to 1501, seems to have been the Portuguese Coelho expedition, except that he claimed this reached as far as 52° south, which would somewhat unbelievably have taken it as far as the Falkland Islands. The fourth, in 1503, seems to have been another minor Portuguese one.

That Vespucci indulged in more than a few lies is quite evident from, for instance, his extravagant mentions of 'lions' in South America. He also pretended to have been the discoverer in charge of the expeditions, effectively as if neither Hojeda nor Coelho had even existed. One totally proven lie is that throughout 1497, the year he claimed to have been away on his otherwise unknown first expedition, there is indisputable documentary evidence to show that he was back home in his native Florence.

However, whereas Columbus went to his death believing his voyages had been to Asia, and no-one can know what Cabot thought he had found as a result of his 1498 voyage, Vespucci, with the undoubted benefit of some genuine exploratory experience behind him, outrightly and indeed percipiently spoke of the transatlantic terrain that he had seen as 'a New World ... a continent more densely peopled and abounding in animals than our Europe or Asia or Africa.'

Furthermore, the lurid and partly genuine detail with which he laced the stories of his travels – reports of cannibalism, and totally naked people living communally in large log houses – ensured that these achieved the widest possible international circulation.

As a result, when in 1507 a young geographer called Martin Waldseemüller was publishing a map of the world according to the latest geographical discoveries, it was to Vespucci that he accredited the discovery of this 'New World', adding in his explanatory text:

Amerigo Vespucci — detail from the Waldseemüller map of 1507.

...in virtue of which I believe it very just that it [the 'New World'] should be named Amerige after its discoverer, Americus... *or let it be America*, since both Europa and Asia bear names of feminine form.

On the map itself Waldseemüller duly inscribed 'America' upon what we now know as the South American continent, thus by one stroke of the pen according Vespucci an honour far greater than even Waldseemüller could ever have appreciated. There has also been more than a little suspicion that the undeniably self-glorifying Vespucci contrived to get himself so honoured. But if so, was there something that gave him the idea?

Here more than a little curious is why it was Vespucci's Christian name that should have been used. In fairness, this may simply have been because *vespucci* means 'wasp' in Italian, the naming of a whole continent 'Waspland' thereby hardly being the most enticing. But there is also the fact that Vespucci deliberately backdated his purported achievement by stating that his first voyage commenced in May 1497. Why did he choose the very date of John Cabot's departure on the voyage that *genuinely* first discovered the north American mainland?

Even more curious, however – and at the very least the most extraordinary coincidence – is a name to be found on the Westminster Abbey accounts roll that records the payment of the £20 pension that King Henry VII granted Cabot. This payment – dated 1498, a year before Vespucci had even begun his first genuine voyage – was made from Bristol's customs receipts, and thereby bears the names of the two collectors responsible for directly handing this money to Cabot and his family.

The name of Richard Ameryk — detail from the Bristol customs roll in Westminster Abbey.

One of these is 'Arthur Kemys', of mere passing interest as possibly the brother of the John Kemys to whom Cabot paid the rent for his St Nicholas Street home.

Far more startling, however, is the name of the other 'Richard Ameryk'. Ameryk was a wealthy Bristol merchant who made his money by investing in trading

The 'Americ' merchant mark of Richard Ameryk.

voyages, also by buying-up local lands, in the course of which, according to as yet unpublished researches by archaeologist Colin Godman, he used some highly unpleasant bully-boy methods on his tenant farmers. In the village of Long Ashton, to the west of Bristol, there survive parts of a farmhouse, Lower Court Farm, which Ameryk purchased for his daughter Joan and her husband John Brook, later a serjeant-at-law under Henry VIII.

But the inevitable fascination is the close association of the name 'Ameryk' with that of John Cabot, discoverer of North America. This is further heightened by the fact that the spelling of the name on Ameryk's merchant mark, at a time when the spelling of names was non-standardised, was actually 'Americ'. Ambassador Soncino, in his report about Cabot, had specifically remarked on Cabot's fondness for grand gestures, such as promising a whole island to his Bristol barber. So might he have been disposed to make a similar gesture for the powerful Bristol magnate who paid him his pension – if not the naming of a whole continent, at least perhaps a substantial chunk of it?

Here one scenario that cannot altogether be ignored is the possibility that on the charts that Hojeda and La Cosa arguably captured from the remnants of Cabot's 1498 expedition, Cabot or whoever was continuing the mapping had named a suitably impressive expanse of territory 'America' in honour of his Bristolian paymaster. Whereupon did the vain and unscrupulous Vespucci, looking over Hojeda and La Cosa's shoulders, seeing this and recognizing the closeness of it to his own Christian name, perhaps get the idea of having this whole 'New World' named after himself? Might he have deliberately dated his fictitious first voyage to the time of Cabot's 1497 expedition specifically to blur the lines of truth, and reinforce his claim?

In the present state of our knowledge, all this is far too tenuous for it to be offered as anything but a suggestion. But at the very least, this association of the discoverer of North America with a Bristol merchant called Richard Ameryk has to be one of the most remarkable of coincidences...

Medieval chantry chapel still surviving at Long Ashton, Bristol, where Ameryk purchased lands for his daughter Joan and son-in-law John Brook.

THE CABOT LEGACY

ELUSIVE AS THE evidence may seem for John Cabot and his men even having survived the 1498 transatlantic crossing, let alone having reached as far as South America, the distinguished historian Dr Alwyn Ruddock has been working on quite independent researches suggesting that John Cabot *did* somehow eventually manage to re-cross the Atlantic back to Bristol, wherever he may have been in the interim. Although Dr Ruddock's findings have yet to be published, her argument is that Cabot may have become a member of a syndicate that was quite definitely involved in voyages to the 'new found land' between 1502 and 1505, returning with a red painted bow and arrows, hawks, 'popynjays' (seemingly small parrots – possibly the Carolina Paroquet), and other souvenirs. There can be no doubt of these voyages, during which native Americans 'clothed in animal skins' were also shipped back to Bristol and then taken to Henry VII's court in London.

And if it had not already started, the Newfoundland cod industry also must have begun at around this time. As the sixteenth century wore on so many ships regularly crossed the Atlantic for this purpose that there was a serious dried fish shortage when these became requisitioned for fighting the Spanish Armada. Certainly by the early seventeenth century 250 West Country vessels were engaged on the Newfoundland dried fish run.

There can also be absolutely no doubt that Cabot's son Sebastian lived on, apparently not having accompanied his father on the 1498 expedition. He and remaining members of the family seem to have stayed in Bristol for some years, for on a Bristol customs roll for 1505 'Sebastian Caboot Venetian' features for the first time receiving a pension of £10 from King Henry VII, to be paid, as his father's had been, from the port of Bristol's customs receipts.

It would also appear that, whatever his father's fate, Sebastian was undeterred from following in his footsteps as a transatlantic explorer. He quite definitely made a journey to North America under the English flag in 1508-9, his wanderings having been sufficiently far north to encounter icebergs in July and continuous daylight. He also coasted the eastern seaboard, though because no log or first-hand description by him has survived, the exact details are sketchy.

From around 1512, England seeming to have no further use for him under the young Henry VIII, Sebastian changed his allegiance to Spain. In this service he became employed as chief pilot and keeper of the *padrón real*, the official map of the West Indies, on which plans for all Spanish transatlantic voyages were based. In 1526 Sebastian led an expedition under the Spanish flag to the River Plate in South America, and he continued in Spanish service to 1548. But he is known definitely to have returned to England for the last decade of his life, being described at this point as ' a man ... very renowned' whose advice was sought on various exploration projects. By which time, although we do not know the exact year of his birth, he must have been at least seventy.

There have been some accusations that Sebastian played down and even deliberately lied about his father, claiming that he had died in 1492, and that it was he, Sebastian, who led the expedition of 1497. But since this derives mostly from second-hand information that a Mantuan gentleman imparted to a Venetian enthusiast for discovery voyages, the fault may lie in garbled transmission rather than any real ill intentions on the part of Sebastian himself.

Even so, during his long life Sebastian ought to have had ample opportunity to publicise his father's achievements. Yet he omitted to do so. Since he set down little enough record of his own, such failure may well have been a genetic trait, though in Sebastian's case destruction of his maps and manuscripts was also at least partly to blame. For instance we know that there were manuscript maps of his in the Palace of Whitehall late in the sixteenth century; also that his friend and executor William Worthington had more maps and writings by him that survived at least up to 1582.

But although the intention had been for these to be published by Hakluyt, they have long disappeared. The main surviving map which he had some hand in is a printed world map of 1544, of which there remains just a single copy in the Bibliothèque Nationale, Paris. A work of Sebastian's old age, and with various constraints due to the 'classified' nature of cartographical details learned in government service, it tells us little.

Sebastian Cabot died in 1557, and although he is known to have had a daughter, Elizabeth, the number of present-day individuals bearing the name Cabot, and claiming to be part of John and Sebastian Cabot's lineage, is rather greater than the evidence for their descent. One branch of the family certainly settled in Jersey after the Civil War, during which they had supported the Royalists. Others emigrated to America (where the Cabots of Boston are legendary), also Canada and New Zealand. Those who stayed in St Helier, Jersey, have claimed the most direct descent, among these Philip Cabot, born in 1900, who when he visited Bristol in his seventies was noted to bear the

Sebastian Cabot, after a lost contemporary portrait.

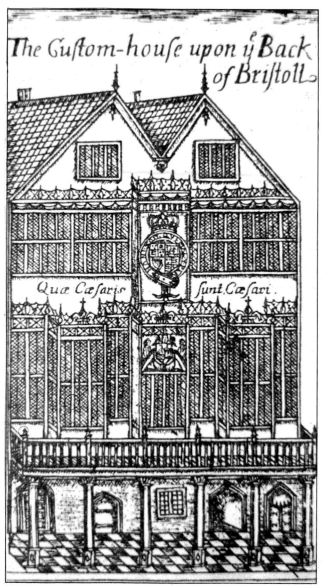

The Bristol Customs House, from a seventeenth-century engraving.

most striking facial resemblance to the only known portrait of Sebastian Cabot, preserved via an engraving.

John Cabot's ship *The Matthew* may also have survived for some years after its historic transatlantic crossing in 1497. There is no known evidence that it was used for the 1498 expedition. Conversely, Bristol's customs records for 1503-4, the first to survive after 1497, certainly include entries for a 'bark' called *The Matthew* busily plying between Ireland, Bristol and Bordeaux, and this continued to be featured for some years after this.

Whether or not this was Cabot's historic ship, of its eventual fate there is no record, for during the 1500s, no-one would have given a second thought to the possibility that Englishmen living at the turn of the twenty- first century might be interested in what it looked like. But with the five hundredth anniversary of John Cabot's voyage of 1497, that interest has certainly been kindled, to the extent even of the building of an actual life-size replica of *The Matthew*, scheduled to repeat John Cabot's epic voyage in 1997.

So how has the twentieth century *Matthew* been created?

THE BUILDING OF
THE MATTHEW RECONSTRUCTION

I N MARCH 1994, four hundred and ninety-seven years
after the first *Matthew's* departure on Cabot's voyage
of 1497, some already carefully selected timber was
delivered to Bristol's Redcliffe Quay for the building of
a full-size reconstruction of *The Matthew*. From drawings prepared by the naval architect Colin Mudie, a
twelve-man team of ship-wrights led by project
manager Mike Blackwell set to work to translate the
timber into a sea-worthy vessel capable of safely
crossing the Atlantic, just as the first *Matthew* had done.

To create his drawings of the new *Matthew* Colin Mudie
reviewed all available information – medieval paintings
and documents, underwater archaeological finds from
shipwrecks, early ship models, his own experience as a
ship-builder, etc. – in order to arrive at his best possible
guess at what *The Matthew* may have looked like. No-
one can be sure that his very shapely design exactly
resembles the original *Matthew*. Some would argue that
the original, most likely designed to sit Bristol-fashion
on the Avon mud, may well have been more like a
barge or a Severn trow.

Whatever, there can be little doubt that the new
Matthew has been built every bit as strong and sea-
worthy as Cabot's original craft, even if not all materials are exactly as the medieval ship-builders would
have used. For instance, although the original keel was
almost certainly of oak or elm, for the reconstruction
Mike Blackwell selected a forty-eight foot long piece of
opepe, an African hardwood. This was because

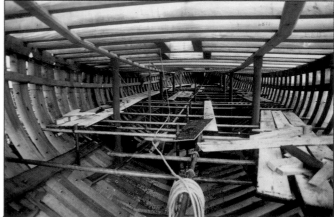

The Matthew *replica under construction on*
Redcliffe Quay, Bristol.

Vital work: the job of caulking The Matthew*, inserting the tarred rope between the ship's planks to make it watertight. This task occupied three men for three full weeks.*

back-bone. Opepe is not an endangered species, and Blackwell's choice of the particular specimen used was because it was straight, true, and the best piece of timber he could find for the job. Shaped to a keel 13 inches wide by 15 inches deep, it weighs 2 ¹/₂ tons.

Opepe was also used for the beams, but with these exceptions, most of the new *Matthew's* remaining structural timbers are of English oak, about 20 trees being used in total, all grown within 40 miles radius of Bristol. Seasoning for more than six years was necessary for the oak selected for stem and stern posts, the stem being the foremost timber into which all the planks are fastened, and the stern post the aftmost part of the hull, on which the rudder is hung. Each of these comprises two oak pieces which have been 'scarfed' together by skilful carpentry, then in turn scarfed onto the keel. For the ribs, however, each of which have to be sawn to the shape of the ship's side, unseasoned oak was deemed serviceable enough, as the wood is much easier to work when 'green', and medieval ship-builders are thought to have chosen likewise, since ribs can readily season while in situ.

To bolt together the timbers comprising the ribs the original *Matthew's* builders almost certainly used wooden nails known as 'tree nails' or 'trunnels' but for reasons of durability Mike Blackwell and his team chose bolts made of aluminium bronze, and similar modern metals for other fastenings. Thus the oak and larch planks around the sides, each one specially steamed in a sealed box to help bend it into the right shape, have been nailed in position using silicon bronze dump nails, while silicon bronze barbed nails have been chosen for the decking.

For keeping the ship watertight, however, the well-tried traditional methods of 'caulking' were used as the most

England no longer has any elm or oak of sufficient length and quality for what is quite literally the ship's

historically correct and effective. For this tarred hemp, or oakum, was hammered into each gap between the planking. With the natural swelling of the planks on contact with the water, an excellent water-tight seal is created.

Launched on September 9, 1995, *The Matthew* was next to be given rigging, masts and sails, followed by sea-trials, in preparation for her commissioning at the International Festival of the Sea held in Bristol from 24 to 27 May 1996. Then in 1997 she will cross the Atlantic to Newfoundland. On 24 June 1997 the Premier of Canada with representatives from England and Italy are scheduled to watch *The Matthew* sail into St John's harbour. Whether or not it was St John's that Cabot reached on that date, she will certainly thus commemorate the exact five hundredth aniversary of John Cabot's historic voyage. Then, after a tour of the eastern seaboard of the United States, she will return to a permanent berth in Bristol, as is only right and fitting.

The mainmast under construction early in 1996. When completed, the reconstructed ship would have three masts — two with square sails and the aft with a more conventional sail called the mizzen.

The scene shortly before the official launching by Lady Wills on 9 September, 1995. Mindful of Bristol's sherry connections, Lady Wills broke a bottle of Bristol Cream sherry instead of the traditional champagne. In 1997, the ship will repeat Cabot's voyage to Newfoundland, 500 years after his historic discovery.

The Matthew *afloat during its trials in March, 1996. In the background is St Mary Redcliffe church, one of Bristol's medieval buildings which Cabot would recognize today.*

In the Avon Gorge, with Brunel's Suspension Bridge behind.

FURTHER READING

Baddely St. Clair, 'A Bristol Rental, 1498-9' *Transactions of the Bristol and Gloucestershire Archaeological Society*, vol XLVII, 1925, pp.123-9.

Bryan Little, *John Cabot: The Reality*, Bristol, Redcliffe Press, 1983.

Samuel E. Morison, *The European Discovery of America: Vol I, The Northern Voyages, AD 500-1600*, Oxford University Press, 1971.

David B. Quinn, *England and the Discovery of America*, London, Allen & Unwin, 1974.

David B. Quinn, *Sebastian Cabot and Bristol Exploration*, Bristol Branch of the Historical Association, revised edition, 1993.

Alwyn A. Ruddock, 'John Day of Bristol and the English Voyages across the Atlantic before 1497', *Geographical Journal*, 132, 1966, pp.225-33.

James A. Williamson (ed.), *The Cabot Voyages and Bristol Discovery under Henry VII*, Hakluyt Society, 2nd series no.CXX, 1962.

Ian Wilson, *The Columbus Myth: Did Men of Bristol Reach America before Columbus?*, London, Simon & Schuster, 1991.

ACKNOWLEDGEMENTS

The text of this book has been partly adapted from my *The Columbus Myth: Did men of Bristol reach America before Columbus?*, published by Simon and Schuster, London, 1991. I am particularly grateful to Vanessa Evans, Mrs St John Hartnell, John and Angela Sansom of The Redcliffe Press and Steven Pugsley of Westcountry Books for their enthusiastic support by which this present publication came into being, also to Penny Samuels, formerly of the Matthew Visitor Centre and Mike Blackwell of the Matthew Project for their kindness in introducing me to the new *Matthew* while this was still an early stage of its construction.

The photographs reproduced were either taken by myself, or as follows: p.4, courtesy Bristol City Museums and Art Gallery; p.6, Spanish National Archives, Simancas, Spain; p.10, courtesy Bristol Record Office; p.17, courtesy National Portrait Gallery, London; p.24, Donald McCleod; p.28, Bill Bishop; p.34, G.Bradley/ The Town of Bonavista, Newfoundland; pp.41 and 61 (top), courtesy Dean and Chapter of Westminster Abbey; pp.54-5 and 56, National Geographic Magazine and the Naval Museum, Madrid, Spain; p.60, courtesy Schuler Verlag, W. Germany. The maps reproduced on p.9, p.37 and p.49 have been supplied courtesy of Simon & Schuster, London. I should also like to thank David Redfern of the Festival of the Sea/Matthew Project for providing photographs of the *Matthew* replica under construction and on its sea trials.

Ian Wilson
April 1996